EARLY CHILDHOOD EDUCATION SERIES
Leslie R. Williams, Editor Millie Almy, Senior Advisor

ADVISORY BOARD: Barbara T. Bowman, Harriet K. Cuffaro, Stephanie Feeney, Doris Pronin Fromberg, Celia Genishi, Stacie G. Goffin, Dominic F. Gullo, Alice Sterling Honig, Elizabeth Jones, Gwen Morgan, David Weikart

Inside a Head Start Center:
Developing Policies from Practice
DEBORAH CEGLOWSKI

Uncommon Caring: Learning from Men
Who Teach Young Children
JAMES R. KING

Teaching and Learning in a Diverse World:
Multicultural Education for Young
Children, 2nd Ed.
PATRICIA G. RAMSEY

Windows on Learning:
Documenting Young Children's Work
JUDY HARRIS HELM, SALLEE BENEKE,
& KATHY STEINHEIMER

Bringing Reggio Emilia Home:
An Innovative Approach to
Early Childhood Education
LOUISE BOYD CADWELL

Major Trends and Issues in Early
Childhood Education: Challenges
Controversies, and Insights
JOAN P. ISENBERG & MARY RENCK JALONGO, Eds.

Master Players:
Learning from Children at Play
GRETCHEN REYNOLDS & ELIZABETH JONES

Understanding Young Children's Behavior:
A Guide for Early Childhood Professionals
JILLIAN RODD

Understanding Quantitative and Qualitative
Research in Early Childhood Education
WILLIAM L. GOODWIN & LAURA D. GOODWIN

Diversity in the Classroom:
New Approaches to the Education
of Young Children, 2nd Ed.
FRANCES E. KENDALL

Developmentally Appropriate Practice
in "Real Life": Stories of Teacher
Practical Knowledge
CAROL ANNE WIEN

Quality in Family Child Care
and Relative Care
SUSAN KONTOS, CAROLLEE HOWES,
MARYBETH SHINN, & ELLEN GALINSKY

Using the Supportive Play Model:
Individualized Intervention in Early
Childhood Practice
MARGARET K. SHERIDAN,
GILBERT M. FOLEY, & SARA H. RADLINSKI

The Full-Day Kindergarten:
A Dynamic Themes Curriculum, 2nd Ed.
DORIS PRONIN FROMBERG

Experimenting with the World: John Dewey
and the Early Childhood Classroom
HARRIET K. CUFFARO

New Perspectives in Early Childhood
Teacher Education: Bringing
Practitioners into the Debate
STACIE G. GOFFIN & DAVID E. DAY, Eds.

Assessment Methods for Infants and
Toddlers: Transdisciplinary Team
Approaches
DORIS BERGEN

The Emotional Development of Young
Children: Building an Emotion-Centered
Curriculum
MARION C. HYSON

Young Children Continue to Reinvent
Arithmetic–3rd Grade: Implications of
Piaget's Theory
CONSTANCE KAMII with SALLY JONES LIVINGSTON

Moral Classrooms, Moral Children:
Creating a Constructivist Atmosphere in
Early Education
RHETA DeVRIES & BETTY ZAN

Diversity and Developmentally Appropriate
Practices: Challenges for Early Childhood
Education
BRUCE L. MALLORY & REBECCA S. NEW, Eds.

Understanding Assessment and Evaluation
in Early Childhood Education
DOMINIC F. GULLO

Changing Teaching, Changing Schools:
Bringing Early Childhood Practice
into Public Education–Case Studies
from the Kindergarten
FRANCES O'CONNELL RUST

(Continued)

D1118392

Early Childhood Education Series titles, continued

Physical Knowledge in Preschool
Education: Implications of Piaget's Theory
CONSTANCE KAMII & RHETA DeVRIES

Caring for Other People's Children:
A Complete Guide to Family Day Care
FRANCES KEMPER ALSTON

Family Day Care: Current Research for
Informed Public Policy
DONALD L. PETERS & ALAN R. PENCE, Eds.

The Early Childhood Curriculum:
A Review of Current Research, 2nd Ed.
CAROL SEEFELDT, Ed.

Reconceptualizing the Early Childhood
Curriculum: Beginning the Dialogue
SHIRLEY A. KESSLER &
BETH BLUE SWADENER, Eds.

Ways of Assessing Children and Curriculum:
Stories of Early Childhood Practice
CELIA GENISHI, Ed.

The Play's the Thing:
Teachers' Roles in Children's Play
ELIZABETH JONES & GRETCHEN REYNOLDS

Scenes from Day Care: How Teachers
Teach and What Children Learn
ELIZABETH BALLIETT PLATT

Raised in East Urban: Child Care Changes
in a Working Class Community
CAROLINE ZINSSER

United We Stand: Collaboration for Child
Care and Early Education Services
SHARON L. KAGAN

Making Friends in School: Promoting Peer
Relationships in Early Childhood
PATRICIA G. RAMSEY

Play and the Social Context of
Development in Early Care and Education
BARBARA SCALES, MILLIE ALMY,
AGELIKI NICOLOPOULOU, &
SUSAN ERVIN-TRIPP, Eds.

The Whole Language Kindergarten
SHIRLEY RAINES & ROBERT CANADY

Children's Play and Learning:
Perspectives and Policy Implications
EDGAR KLUGMAN & SARA SMILANSKY

Serious Players in the Primary Classroom:
Empowering Children Through Active
Learning Experiences
SELMA WASSERMANN

Multiple Worlds of Child Writers:
Friends Learning to Write
ANNE HAAS DYSON

Young Children Continue to Reinvent
Arithmetic—2nd Grade: Implications
of Piaget's Theory
CONSTANCE KAMII

Literacy Learning in the Early Years:
Through Children's Eyes
LINDA GIBSON

The Good Preschool Teacher:
Six Teachers Reflect on Their Lives
WILLIAM AYERS

A Child's Play Life: An Ethnographic Study
DIANA KELLY-BYRNE

Professionalism and the
Early Childhood Practitioner
BERNARD SPODEK, OLIVIA N. SARACHO,
& DONALD L. PETERS, Eds.

Looking at Children's Play:
The Bridge from Theory to Practice
PATRICIA A. MONIGHAN-NOUROT,
BARBARA SCALES, JUDITH L. VAN HOORN, &
MILLIE ALMY

The War Play Dilemma:
Balancing Needs and Values in
the Early Childhood Classroom
NANCY CARLSSON-PAIGE & DIANE E. LEVIN

The Piaget Handbook for Teachers and
Parents: Children in the Age of Discovery,
Preschool–3rd Grade
ROSEMARY PETERSON &
VICTORIA FELTON-COLLINS

Promoting Social and Moral
Development in Young Children
CAROLYN POPE EDWARDS

Today's Kindergarten
BERNARD SPODEK, Ed.

Supervision in Early Childhood Education
JOSEPH J. CARUSO & M. TEMPLE FAWCETT

Visions of Childhood:
Influential Models from Locke to Spock
JOHN CLEVERLEY & D. C. PHILLIPS

Starting School:
From Separation to Independence
NANCY BALABAN

Young Children Reinvent Arithmetic:
Implications of Piaget's Theory
CONSTANCE KAMII

Ideas Influencing Early Childhood
Education: A Theoretical Analysis
EVELYN WEBER

The Joy of Movement in Early Childhood
SANDRA R. CURTIS

Inside
a Head Start
Center

DEVELOPING POLICIES
FROM PRACTICE

Deborah Ceglowski

FOREWORD BY DANIEL J. WALSH

Teachers College, Columbia University
New York and London

Published by Teachers College Press, 1234 Amsterdam Avenue, New York, NY 10027

Copyright © 1998 by Teachers College, Columbia University

All rights reserved. No part of this publication may be reproduced or transmitted in any form or by any means, electronic or mechanical, including photocopy, or any information storage and retrieval system, without permission from the publisher

An earlier version of Chapter 6 appeared under the title "Writing Short Stories" in *Children in Context: Theories, Methods, and Ethics,* edited by M. E. Graue and D. J. Walsh, pp. 228–238, copyright © 1998 by Sage Publications. Adapted by permission of Sage Publications.

An earlier version of the Preface, the opening vignette of Chapter 1, and Chapter 9 appeared under the title "That's a Good Story, But Is It Really Research?" in *Qualitative Inquiry, 3*(2), 188–201 (1997), copyright © 1997 by Sage Publications. Adapted by permission of Sage Publications.

Library of Congress Cataloging-in-Publication Data

Ceglowski, Deborah.
 Inside a Head Start center : developing policies from practice / Deborah Ceglowski ; foreword by Daniel J. Walsh.
  p.   cm.—(Early childhood education series)
 Includes bibliographical references (p.   ) and index.
 ISBN 0-8077-3748-8 (paper : alk. paper).—ISBN 0-8077-3749-6 (cloth : alk. paper)
  1. Head Start programs—United States—Case studies.   2. Socially handicapped children—Education (Preschool)—United States—Case studies.   3. Education, Rural—United States—Case studies.   4. Education and state—United States—Case studies.
 5. School management and organization—United States—Case studies.   I. Title.
 II. Series: Early childhood education series (Teachers College Press)
 LC4069.2.C45   1998
 372.21—dc21   98-17077

ISBN 0-8077-3748-8 (paper)
ISBN 0-8077-3749-6 (cloth)

Printed on acid-free paper
Manufactured in the United States of America

05 04 03 02 01 00 99 98   8 7 6 5 4 3 2 1

To the memory of my aunt, Ruth Thibodeau

In these messy and idiosyncratic staff stories, we may,
if we listen closely enough, hear visions of policy.
—*From Chapter 12*

Contents

Foreword by Daniel J. Walsh   *xiii*

Preface   *xv*

Acknowledgments   *xxi*

PART I
Practice and Context

1   Framing the Study   3

    Studying the Connection Between Head Start Policy and
      Program Quality   *6*
    Refocusing on the Local Perspective   *9*
    Conclusion   *13*

2   The Development of Head Start   15

    Planning for Head Start   *18*
    Head Start Begins   *20*
    Waning Support for Head Start   *21*
    Head Start Focuses on Improvement   *21*
    Head Start Expands   *23*
    Summary   *25*

3   Looking at the Hoover Community Action Corporation and
    Wood River Head Start   27

    Hoover CAC Head Start   *28*
    Wood River Head Start   *30*
    The Federal Inspection of Wood River   *33*
    Understanding the Context of Head Start   *34*

PART II
Windows on Policy

4 The Move to the Early Learning Center   41

   Relocating Head Start   *43*
   The Dailiness of Wood River Head Start   *46*
   Examining Policy Implications   *53*

5 Research as Relationship: The Wood River Head Start Families   59

   The Head Start Children and Their Families   *62*
   Parent Participation at Wood River   *66*
   Examining Policy Implications   *68*

6 Developing Policies from Practice: The Story of Mark,
   the Finicky Eater   73

   Eating Policies   *75*
   Defining Mark as a Finicky Eater   *76*
   Developing a Policy from Practice   *78*
   Examining Policy Implications   *81*

7 Official Policies and Working Policies   85

   Need for Official Policies   *87*
   Learning About Head Start Policies   *88*
   Emphasizing or Downplaying Policies   *89*
   Examining Policy Implications   *90*

8 Developing Practices and Tiny Tales of Success   92

   The Practice of Collocation   *95*
   The Practice of Cooperative Programming   *99*
   Examining Policy Implications   *104*

9 Establishing Policy Priorities   109

   Local-Match Policy   *110*
   Examining Policy Implications   *114*

10 Understanding Policies Through Relationships   119

   Child Abuse Reporting Policies   *122*
   Defining Jasmine as an Abuse Victim   *123*

Meeting with Jasmine's Mother   *123*
Helping Jasmine's Healing Process   *125*
Examining Policy Implications   *127*

11 Conclusion   130

How Is Policy Defined in a Local Program?   *131*
How Do Staff Interpret and Negotiate Official Policies?   *132*
How Do Local Staff Negotiate Policies and Local Needs?   *137*
How Do Staff Develop Local Policies?   *140*
Lessons from Wood River   *141*

Epilogue   *147*

References   *149*

Index   *157*

About the Author   *165*

Foreword

Today, when I think about policy, I think in terms of constraints on decisionmaking. Back when I was a teacher, I thought about being told what to do and what not to do.

I spent the late 1960s and the 1970s teaching young children, mostly poor, mostly Black. For a while, I was a Head Start teacher. Later, I taught at a Child-Parent Center, an offshoot of Head Start, on Chicago's West Side.

I once worked in a program where men teachers were not allowed to accompany the girls, as young as 2, into the bathrooms. My coworkers said this was progress—until the year before, men had not been allowed to work with preschoolers at all. A fellow male teacher whose principal let him work with preschoolers despite the policy described how he hid from a supervisor in a closet on a surprise visit while his assistant pretended she was the teacher.

Policy came from "up there and far away," passed down through countless layers of desk folks until it arrived at my classroom on the West Side of Chicago. Three things I was sure of: No one had asked me about what was needed; the policy wasn't going to make my life easier; and no one cared what I thought about it anyway.

Policies arrived regularly, usually announced by the principal at meetings or over the intercom. They were always critically important and had to be implemented immediately lest dire consequences result. Given the many layers between our little center and the Feds and the Chicago Board of Education, who knew how old and how filtered the newly arrived policy was? Chances were another one was already winding its inexorable way down, to replace the one presently disrupting our lives and disrupt them in new ways.

The Child-Parent Centers were test driven (remember, this was the post–Westinghouse Report era). Our funding, our jobs, we were constantly reminded, depended on high test scores. We had the usual scheduled tests, but we also had unscheduled tests.

One year an unscheduled test materialized two weeks before Christmas, a fine time to test 3-, 4-, and 5-year-olds. It had to be given immediately— our future depended on it. The test took most of the week, and a lot of the holiday spirit.

A month later, I was waiting to talk to the principal. The office was crowded with file cabinets and boxes. Absentmindedly I removed a large envelope wedged between some boxes; out of idle curiosity I looked inside. I found the absolutely-necessary-to-our-future pre-Christmas tests, each classroom's neatly paperclipped together. I was rather upset, but I calmed myself and replaced the envelope just as the principal called me in.

I think I intended to pull the envelope out the next time a surprise test arrived. I don't remember actually doing so. I do remember checking on the envelope every week or so for a while. Maybe it's still there. We didn't lose our funding or our jobs.

Researchers have been studying policy for years. Colleges of Education have policy departments and centers for the study of policy. But what we know about policy is up there and far away. As close as we get to the classroom in the ghetto is a questionnaire. I remember filling out questionnaires about whether I was doing what I was supposed to be doing. I always was.

In this book, Deb Ceglowski writes about here and close, about one Head Start center and the people there. She describes how they deal with the demands on their lives and how they do what they do here and close despite everything from up there and far away.

Deb has written an important book. After a hundred years of educational research, we are still figuring out that to understand schools, we have to go into those schools and spend a lot of time being there.

Deb Ceglowski did that. She became part of the Wood River Head Start. She writes about it in riveting detail and with uncommon power. She writes about policy from the other side, from down here and very close.

No one ever did that about my classroom on the West Side of Chicago.

Daniel J. Walsh
University of Illinois at Urbana-Champaign

Preface

From September 1993 to May 1995, I joined the four-member staff of a Head Start program as a volunteer to study how policies and mandates are enacted in the day-to-day lives of Head Start staff. Using qualitative methods of participant observation, field notes, discussions with staff and administrators, and analysis of local and federal Head Start policies, I aimed to understand how staff interpret and implement official policies within the context of mundane and extraordinary events at the program. Currently there are no other studies examining policy from the perspective of the experiences of Head Start staff.

My interest in Head Start policy began years ago when I developed and implemented training programs for Head Start staff in several midwestern states. Administrators and teachers complained that the amount of paperwork required by the federal government had dramatically increased and that this interfered with their efforts to provide services to families and children.

My first acquaintance with Hoover Community Action Corporation (CAC) Head Start* occurred in 1985 when the former Head Start director called and asked if I would conduct a workshop on puppet making. During the past 10 years my activities with Hoover CAC have included teaching college courses, consulting with teachers and staff regarding problem situations, serving on the Health Advisory Council, and designing and facilitating in-service training sessions for the staff. My responsibilities have included advising Hoover CAC Head Start staff working toward an early childhood education credential. In 1990 I served as Paula Walsh's early childhood advisor. Paula, a Hoover CAC Head Start aide, completed her early childhood program during her last session of chemotherapy treatment for breast cancer. The picture taken to commemorate the day on which she successfully passed the final evaluation shows her hairless head wrapped in a paisley scarf. Two months later I received a call that Paula had died. Perhaps Paula's gift to me

---

*Names of agencies, places, and individuals in the study are pseudonyms.

was the understanding that one can continue to work toward a long-term goal in the face of certain death. I now think that her courageous last days provided the first seeds of my thinking that the administrators and staff of this Head Start program, with whom I had worked for 10 years, were the very ones whom I wanted to study for my dissertation project.

In the fall of 1992 I wrote to Ann Norstrom, the Head Start director, asking her if I could do my dissertation on the Hoover CAC Head Start program. I explained my interest in studying the impact of Head Start policies on the daily lives of Head Start staff. I asked for permission to spend at least one year at a Head Start center, preferably as a paid aide. My decision to enter a program as an aide was influenced by my relationships with Norman Denzin and Beth Graue.

Denzin (1994) encourages researchers to find what is naturally occurring in the group studied. Researchers are to enter the "lived experience" of those they study, to collect the stories told on the site, and to discover how the group defines the phenomena under investigation. In this research version, researchers make themselves available for interactions with those studied to form relationships and friendships and to listen to the stories told and retold at the research site. Graue (1993) describes her own research stance of working as an aide from two perspectives: joining the school community and sharing her own skills. She explains that by taking the role of aide she participated in the daily interchanges among teachers and children. She also knew that in her former role as a kindergarten teacher she would be uncomfortable observing in a kindergarten classroom. Graue understood that it was through interactions with the kindergarten teachers and children whom she studied that she would develop her understanding of kindergarten readiness.

I was convinced that it was in conversations with the staff, on the bus routes, during breakfast, on the playground, and before and after school, that I would learn how staff interpret official policies to meet the compliance requirements of Hoover CAC and the needs of the families and children served. I waited for Ann to answer my letter. After 2 months, she had not responded, so I followed up with several phone calls. Ann was reluctant at first. She asked, "What are you looking for? Are you coming to evaluate us? Do we get to comment on what you write?" Before my next phone call, Hoover CAC received notification of the results of a triennial federal evaluation, called a peer review, that had been conducted during the previous fall. The Head Start program met or exceeded federal standards.

Shortly after Ann received the positive news about the peer review, I spoke with her. She now seemed more open to my idea of doing research on Hoover CAC Head Start. I discussed with her either entering a program as a volunteer or applying for the job of aide. I thought that the latter position, with its more limited work hours and responsibilities, would be ideal and that staff membership might provide a more holistic view of the day-to-day events of the program. Ann was reluctant to hire me as an aide. "After all," she said, "I know you won't be there more than a year."

The educational component manager, Martha Calle, spoke with Ann in support of my aide application. She cited the current high turnover rate of aides and said that she felt that it was unfair for Hoover CAC to dismiss my application on those grounds. Ann finally agreed to let me submit an aide application to the agency.

When a site aide position opened up early in the summer of 1993, Martha called me for an interview. The opening was at Wood River, one of the Head Start programs operated by Hoover CAC. The site aide's primary responsibilities are to ride the bus for two morning and two afternoon routes of one hour each, wash the dishes, serve the lunch, and clean the kitchen and lunch room.

There were two advantages to studying Head Start policy at Wood River. First, the program was moving from St. John's Catholic School into a public school early childhood center. As I heard the Head Start administrators and teachers discuss the negotiations with the public school personnel, I sensed that the upcoming year would provide rich material for investigating how Head Start staff enact institutional policies in this multiprogram site. For, as Norman Denzin says, it is in times of change, or epiphanic moments, that the underlying structures are most likely to be visible. In addition, Judy Roberts, the Wood River Head Start teacher, was a former Head Start parent, volunteer, aide, and assistant teacher. Her broad-based and extended experience with Head Start would be an asset to my understanding of policies and of the program's history.

Martha Calle, Judy Roberts, and a former Head Start parent, Kathryn Shay, constituted the interviewing team. After some initial questions that established my understanding of Head Start and its policies, Kathryn turned to me and asked, "Why are you applying for this position, with all your qualifications? This job pays $5.00 an hour."

I fumbled for a minute and then responded, "I really believe in Head Start and the program and would like to be part of what goes on."

When I finished, Martha explained that during this year I would be writing my dissertation on Head Start and that as part of this project I would like to work in the program. "However," she continued, "Deb will volunteer her time if she isn't offered the job."

I froze, caught in a researcher's nightmare. Neither the teacher nor the parent had had any notion that I planned to conduct research at this site. Although I intended, at a later date, to reveal my researcher identity to the teacher and parent, I thought that it would be appropriate to wait until I was offered the site aide position.

I do not remember much of what happened after that point in the interview, but I sensed then and there that I would not be offered the job. Later that day, Martha called to confirm that they had offered the job to someone else. Judy, she told me, was more comfortable with someone less experienced and would be "more comfortable with you as a volunteer, not an aide." I felt lucky at that point that Judy would allow me to come as a volunteer!

During the subsequent 2 years the relationships I developed with the Wood River staff and children formed the basis for my understanding of policy mediation and creation. This relational understanding is key to the process of interpreting everyday events and connecting these events to agency and federal policy. I learned about how the staff interpreted and implemented policies by participating in the daily events of the program, including supervising bathroom duty, eating meals with the children and staff, writing accident reports, joining in lesson planning, and attending parent meetings. At the request of staff I substituted as the assistant teacher and site aide. In these capacities I rode the daily bus routes, prepared and served lunches and snacks, and helped in the daily record keeping.

This study was written from the perspective of how the Wood River staff taught me the ways in which policies are interpreted. Most Head Start research has "neglected to document how Head Start program staff adapt to the characteristics, needs, and capabilities of the families they serve" (Phillips & Cabrera, 1996, p. 18). The policy interpretations of staff probably differ from those of administrators and parents because "people involved in Head Start look at it through different perspectives" (Phillips & Cabrera, 1996, p. xii). It is important to understand how staff interpret policy because they provide direct services to families and children.

My written records of this project included 850 pages of field notes, weekly summaries, and monthly calendars depicting events and identifying major themes, and a series of short stories describing the mundane and extraordinary events at the Wood River. I began writing short stories at the beginning of this project because I found that my field notes did not reflect the complexity or drama of the daily events at Wood River. I knew that the short stories provided a more holistic and emotive understanding of these events and, simultaneously, more closely matched the way I was learning about policies. Staff did not talk about policy per se but explained specific policies in the context of daily events. How staff interpreted policy was nested in the daily routines and activities—serving meals, developing the daily schedule, and completing the required paperwork.

Yet I was at a loss as to how I could use the stories as part of the research text. Friend Martha Calle echoed this concern when, after reading the first story I wrote, stopped by my house to return it. She said, "That was a good story. But is that really research?" At the end of my first year at Wood River, in a meeting with my dissertation committee, Norman Denzin, my research director, presented a definition of policy that paved the way for using stories. He stated that policy "is situational; it is open-ended; it is ambiguous; it is ad hoc. It's defined differently by different people depending upon their relationship to what is going on. It's inevitably local and subject to multiple interpretations" (personal communication, June 9, 1994). It was Norman's definition of policy that made me realize that the short stories I wrote could be windows through which to view policy from a local and contextual perspective.

Research short stories employ fictional techniques such as character development, plots, use of dialogue, and strong story line (Van Maanen, 1988). My stories invite the reader into the textual world of Wood River. In the same way that my experiences at the program were cognitive, emotive, and physical, the stories set a narrative framework for readers to know the program in a more holistic way. Stories frame Head Start policy within the context of the daily and mundane events at the program: riding the bus, making meals, filling out paperwork.

Stories provide a different framework for understanding how policies are interpreted in the daily events at a program. I noted in an article that "just as a crystal reflects different colors and patterns, depending upon the viewer's vantage point, different textual representations focus attention on different facets of the topic" (Ceglowski, 1998). Stories broaden our understanding of Head Start policy, which has relied on large-scale studies of policy implementation telling us little about how staff interpret policies.

The Wood River staff was the first reading audience for the 18 stories I wrote and for the drafts of both dissertation and book chapters. Their ongoing critique influenced how I wrote the subsequent chapters and approached revisions. In picking the stories to include in this book, I checked with the staff about the major events that occurred during the 1993–94 year and selected the stories that matched staff's perceptions of that year.

This book is divided into three parts. In Part I, I describe the focus of the study and background information on Head Start, Hoover CAC, and Wood River. Part II consists of the short stories about the Wood River Head Start program. The stories are intended to give the reader a flavor of what it is like to be at Wood River. Sandwiched between the stories is connecting text in which I discuss how the Head Start staff interpret and implement official policies and create policies from practice in relation to the daily activities at Wood River. In Part III, I analyze the policy landscape at Wood River, reexamine the research questions raised in Chapter 1, and suggest new directions for policy research. I conclude by describing in an Epilogue recent developments at Wood River Head Start.

Acknowledgments

This project is rooted in friendships and in the stories that friends have told over the years. I thank first the Wood River Head Start staff: Judy Roberts, Susan Jensen, Ruth Donalds, and Gary Nielson, who welcomed me at Wood River, taught me about Head Start policies, and were first to read the stories. I am grateful to Ann Norstrom for approving this project and to Martha Calle for sharing her Head Start stories as we walked along the Wood River.

Thanks especially to Norman Denzin, my dissertation research director, and Daniel Walsh, my graduate school advisor. Norman was first to encourage me to write stories, and Daniel's support encouraged me to pursue this study. Thank you to Beth Graue for her perspective of how researchers develop relationships with those they study and to Betty Merchant for connecting policy analysis to the daily lives of the Wood River staff.

I would like to thank my friends Marlie Bendiksen, Eileen Borgia, Luci Schueller, Mary Starr Whitney, and Jean Wolf for their valuable insights into this project.

Thank you to Dick Ruppel and Scott Reber of Viterbo College and Susan Liddicoat and Lyn Grossman of Teachers College Press for their invaluable editorial assistance.

Above all, I thank my husband, John Seem, for his support and love. John listened as I unraveled the daily events at Wood River, helped me develop a framework for understanding the stories, and believed in the value of this project.

Finally, I would like to give a special thanks to my children, James and Emily, who helped out at Wood River and at home, enjoyed the stories, and reminded me how stories shift over time.

Inside
a Head Start
Center

DEVELOPING POLICIES
FROM PRACTICE

PART I

Practice and Context

1

Framing the Study

THE WAY TO WOOD RIVER

It's 10:30 A.M. now and time that I'm on my way to the Wood River Head Start program. I take a last sip of hot chocolate and put on my coat, hat, and gloves. The van is outside, warming up, a long tail of exhaust filling the driveway. I run quickly from the house to the van. It's 30 degrees below with the wind chill factor. I head the van out toward the highway, passing the apple stands and glimpsing the river for the last time. The backwaters, filled with dried grass and drifted snow, stretch the six miles from Starr, where I live, to Wood River. I reach the 30-mile-speed-limit sign indicating that Wood River, population 630, is near. The Kwik Trip sign, bright in white and red, is straight on our right. Glancing to the left, I think, "There is the road to Steven's." He is a boy in the Head Start classroom. That country route is cold now, covered in ice and snow.

The van moans as I climb the Wood River hill. St. John's, the only Catholic church in the United States with a fourth floor sanctuary, is there on the right. That's where Head Start was for 25 years. Then, during a federal review, the director was told that the facility was out of compliance with Head Start standards.

The van tops the hill, and Wood River lies ahead, the IGA grocery and the hardware store on the right, and the post office and Wood River Farmer's Cooperative gas station on the left. A few bars are spread in between the buildings. There's the Sidewalk Cafe, just like in Garrison Keillor's stories of Lake Wobegon. At one time there was a lake in the town, and it was a summer resort. Now the lake is gone and the town lingers on, home to 600 residents, mostly farmers.

I put on the left blinker and wait a moment. The oncoming country traffic is tricky. It barrels over the hill, surprising the slower town drivers. I pull around to the back of the school building, passing the upper playground covered with shredded tires. Here's the lower playground and the basketball hoops and the Wood River Early Childhood Center. Contained in the center are three kindergarten rooms, the special education program, the family education program, and the newest arrival, the Head Start program.

The Head Start van is parked near the lower door, delivering the Head Start children. Gary Nielson, the bus driver, stands at the bottom of the stairs, helping the kids. "Careful, now, Philip, don't forget your backpack." He looks my way and tips his Branson (Missouri) cap in greeting. This is the second group of children arriving now, the Hudson and Wood River group. The first arrived an hour ago. Ruth Donalds, the site aide, is handing out the backpacks. She turns toward me and waves, her long brown hair shining in the sun. I park near the fence and head toward the door. The kindergarten children from upstairs crowd into the hall. They are trying to get their coats so they can go home. I make my way down to the end of the hall, where the newly arrived Head Start children are at their hooks, hanging up their coats and backpacks. Sarah spots me; her blue eyes dilate. I smile and say, "Hi, Sarah." She takes my hand and holds it firmly.

Judy Roberts, the teacher, is here helping the children get their coats off and checking their backpacks for notes. "When you finish here, go right into the room," she tells them. This is the first time this morning that the children have been inside the classroom. The children who arrive at 10:00 A.M. eat snack and play in the gym until those from the other program, the one we share the room with, leave at 11.

In the classroom, Susan Jensen, the assistant teacher, is sitting on the carpet near the puzzle area. She answers Luke's call, "I can't do this." She holds out the puzzle pieces, one at a time: "Where do you think this could go?" She and Luke slowly put the puzzle together.

Now Steven is hanging onto my hand, spinning his 4-year-old body around and around. Steven lives with his grandparents and three brothers because his father is a college student in the northern part of the state. His mother left her sons and husband a year ago. "Hey, will ya read a book?" asks Steven. I nod my head in approval. Steven returns with a Clifford book, and the two of us settle on the carpet, near the door to the bathroom.

Judy is at the table near the sink counting the latest batch of parent donations, a collection of dirty one-gallon milk jugs and stacks of egg cartons. The first time I saw this process, I asked, "So what do you do with these things?"

Judy laughed. "Well, most of it ends up in the trash—at least milk jugs and egg cartons like this. We code it in and then dump it." Like all Head Start programs administered by the Hoover CAC, Wood River must submit a monthly verification of parent donations and volunteer services.

Seated at the housekeeping table is 3-year-old Kevin surrounded by a pile of rubber food. Jasmine is cooking at the stove and brings Kevin some more food for thought. "Here, eat this," she tells Kevin, and plops a rubber hot dog on the table. "Remember, at Head Start ya have ta' have it on your plate. You don't have ta' eat it!" At Wood River, even the children understand the policy that stipulates that everyone eating the family-style lunch must put a portion of each food on their plate.

Luke is on the toy phone calling the cops, reporting his own crimes, waiting for the authorities to come and pick him up. Red-haired Mark is lying at Kevin's feet, "playing dead," and Rachel walks by, holding Caleb and Philip by their shirt collars. They both bark at Kevin. He asks Rachel, "Do they bite?"

As the boy-dogs approach, sniffing Kevin's leg, Judy goes to the lights and flicks them on and off, saying, "Time to clean up." We all pitch in, the children and adults. Judy goes to work in the housekeeping area. She straightens up the food spread over the table and in the cupboard. Steven and I straighten out the books. Ruth is there. She helps carry the bags of egg cartons and milk jugs out to the trash. Susan is helping to tidy up the boxes of puzzles that Thomas knocked down when he was trying to put his own away.

During circle time, I sit listening with the children to Susan reading the story about snowmen: "Once there was a boy who wanted to keep his snowman all year round . . . " The children seek out our laps, looking for warm spots, arguing over who will sit where. Today there are practically enough laps for all who would want them. Brian cuddles close to me, and I pull Sarah in close too, putting my arm around her. The day will go on, winding through roll call, bathroom, lunch, tooth brushing, music, and snack. But for now we are all comfortable here, sitting and listening to the story. It is a quiet time to leave the children, the teachers, the program.

The Wood River Head Start program, located in a rural community in the Midwest, is like thousands of other Head Start programs across the United States and its territories. Administered by the Hoover Community Action Corporation, Inc., its mission is to serve families whose incomes fall below the federal poverty guidelines. Since 1965 local Head Start programs, like Wood River, have provided children and families services in four component areas: health, education, social services, and parent involvement. In fiscal year 1997, 146,200 Head Start staff served 752,077 children and their families in 42,500 classrooms located in 16,636 Head Start centers in the United States and territories (U.S. Department of Health and Human Services [U.S. DHHS], 1997).

The early 1990s marked a time of change and rapid growth for Wood River and other Head Start programs. The growth stemmed from two sources. First, research studies such as those of the High Scope Foundation (Barnett & Escobar, 1987; Berrueta-Clement, Schweinhart, Barnett, Epstein, & Weikart, 1984; Schweinhart, Barnes, & Weikart, 1993; Schweinhart & Koshel, 1986; Schweinhart, Koshel, & Bridgman, 1987; Schweinhart & Weikart, 1993) found that quality early childhood programs have significant and long-term impact on the lives of impoverished children, providing a $7 return for each dollar invested in preschool programs. Second, the National Governors Association's recommendations for educational improvement focused attention on the importance of school readiness (U.S. Department of Education, 1991). The first national education goal, "by the year 2000, all children in America will start school ready to learn" (p. 5) spurred new interest in and support for Head Start. Head Start has received bipartisan support for expanding services which has resulted in unprecedented budget increases: from $1.9 billion in FY 1991 to $3.3 billion in FY 1995.

The Head Start Bureau has issued new policy mandates, revised existing policies, and formulated procedures to terminate poorly performing Head Start grantees. The implicit assumption is that more policies and better management will result in higher quality programs.

STUDYING THE CONNECTION BETWEEN HEAD START POLICY AND PROGRAM QUALITY

What, then, is known about the connection between policies and program quality? There are three distinct periods of Head Start policy analysis and research that focus on outcomes for children and families (Collins & Kinney, 1989).

Periods 1 and 2

The first period, 1965–1976, consists of studies of Head Start and other early intervention programs. Researchers answered the question, Do early intervention programs work? The goal of these studies was to determine the effectiveness of Head Start and other early education programs as measured by children's performance in elementary school (Brown, 1978; Datta, McHale, & Mitchell, 1976; Hubbell, 1983; Lazar, Darlington, Murray, Royce, & Snipper, 1982; McKey et al., 1985; Westinghouse Learning Corporation, 1969; Zigler & Anderson, 1979).

The first major evaluation study of Head Start, the Westinghouse Study, was designed to answer the question: "To what extent are the children now in the first, second, and third grades who attended Head Start programs different in their intellectual and social-personal development from comparable children who did not attend?" (Westinghouse, 1969, p. 2) The findings were troubling: Children who attended summer Head Start programs did not maintain cognitive gains through third grade, and those who attended full-year programs maintained only some of the gains through third grade. Moreover, children who attended either summer or full-year programs still tested considerably below national norms (Westinghouse, 1969).

In response to these findings, a group of 12 child development researchers who were investigating experimental preschool and early intervention programs pooled their data and "collaborated in the design of a follow-up study" (Datta, 1982, p. 271). Sheldon White (1968) described these researchers as "experts-turned-advocates." A collaborative research team, the Consortium for Longitudinal Studies, reported that the 12 investigated programs had long-lasting effects in five areas: assignment to special education classes, grade retention, achievement test scores, intelligence test scores, and attitudes and values. All the programs investigated were experimental preschool programs that were staffed with certified teachers and served small numbers of children (Consortium for Longitudinal Studies, 1978, 1983). The research consortium's findings were not transferable to the diverse scope of Head Start programs, but the findings indicated that there was a potential for Head Start programs to achieve such outcomes.

The second period of Head Start policy analysis, 1965–1977, focused on various curricula and service delivery models to determine which are most effective in producing significant and long-lasting gains for Head Start children and their families (Bissell, 1971; Collins, 1980; Coulson, 1972; Love, Nauta, Coelen, Hewlett, & Ruopp, 1976; Lucas, 1975; Nauta & Travers, 1982; M. Smith, 1973; Stanford Research Institute, 1971; Travers, Nauta, & Irwin, 1982). The Head Start Planned Variation Studies found that a variety of curricula and service delivery models are effective in eliciting favorable child outcomes (Datta, 1972, 1982; Miller, 1972; M. Smith, 1973) and that one model of service delivery did not produce significantly better results for children and families than did another model.

These first two periods of Head Start policy analysis assumed "a relatively direct relationship between federal policy 'inputs,' local responses, and program 'outputs'" (McLaughlin, 1990, p. 11); see Figure 1.1.

Although Head Start programs that implement policy may be diverse, the goal of policy implementation was that these programs produce similar, measurable results. Successful policies were those in which the outcomes closely aligned to the original intent of the policy makers. The goal in such a policy model was for consistency in measured outcomes.

Period 3

The third period of Head Start policy analysis, commencing in the mid-1970s and continuing until the present, focuses on the characteristics and indicators of high-quality programs. The direction of this period has been influenced significantly by the Head Start Synthesis Project (McKey et al., 1985), whose authors first reviewed 1,600 research studies conducted from 1965 to 1985 and then employed meta-analysis to analyze the results of 76 of these studies. Meta-analysis is a statistical technique that summarizes the findings of various studies that address the same questions.

The results of the meta-analysis were presented in five categories: cogni-

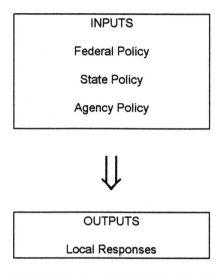

FIGURE 1.1. Input-Output Policy Model

tive development, emotional and social development, health, families, and communities. The Head Start Synthesis Project found

> that children enrolled in Head Start enjoy significant immediate gains in cognitive test scores, socioemotional test scores and health status. In the long run, cognitive and socioemotional test scores of former Head Start students do not remain superior to those of disadvantaged children who did not attend Head Start. However, a small subset of studies find that former Head Starters are more likely to be promoted to the next grade and are less likely to be assigned to special education classes. Head Start has also aided families by providing health, social and educational services and by linking families with services available to the community. (McKey et al., 1985, p. 1)

The Head Start Synthesis Study provided evidence that Head Start has short-term impact on children's growth and development and that some programs may have long-term impact on children's school performance.

In the 1990s Head Start's budget doubled, and with this increase there was growing pressure to document that programs provide high-quality services. Layzer, Goodson, and Moss (1993) found that Head Start programs were among the highest rated when compared to child care and school-sponsored programs. However, studies conducted by the Office of the Inspector General, Health and Human Services (U.S. DHHS, 1993a) and the National Head Start Association (1990) found that some programs did not offer high-caliber services to Head Start children and their families.

In response to the concern about the uneven quality of Head Start programs, the Advisory Committee on Head Start Quality and Expansion (U.S. DHHS, 1993a) recommended that the Head Start research include studies of local Head Start policy issues:

> Although some data is available regarding the quality of Head Start programs, much more information is needed to help plan program improvements and to help inform policy makers about the key elements that lead to program effectiveness. Information is needed at the local and national level that examines the best ways to provide quality services in all components. . . .
>
> The way programs interpret these [Head Start Program Performance] standards to meet the needs of a diverse population under various local conditions can provide a rich source of data regarding how to define and implement comprehensive child development and family support programs. (p. 38)

The research investigating the connection between policies and program quality indicates that various program and curricula models are effective in producing short-term and, in some cases, long-term outcomes for children and families. However, little is known about how programs develop and maintain high-quality services.

One reason for the lack of information about high-quality services is that Head Start programs participating in policy-impact studies are geographically, programmatically, and organizationally distinct. Within such a structural framework, local programs vary in orientation and outcomes. Research studies thus blur the distinctive characteristics of Head Start programs, including how staff develop and maintain daily services to families and young children. Yet it is precisely these distinct differences that determine how each program interprets and implements official polices. As McLaughlin (1990) wrote, "The nature, amount, and pace of change at the local level was a product of local factors that were largely beyond the control of policymakers" (p. 12). It is "local capacity and will" (p. 12) that determine how policies are negotiated at local sites.

REFOCUSING ON THE LOCAL PERSPECTIVE

Historically, Head Start staff, like other teachers, have been overlooked as a source of policy knowledge. One explanation for this may be found in critical feminist literature. Freeman (1988) argues that the development of teaching as nurturance and as women's work is largely responsible for the current system that separates teaching staff as implementers and administrators as policy makers. As Black (1989) notes, teaching provided the vehicle for women to use their nurturing abilities outside the home. It also structured teaching experience along gender lines. Women were viewed as fit to tend to the children, whereas men were suited to hold the positions of authority as superintendent or program administrator.

Freeman (1988) found that teachers have institutionalized this "caring" discourse and think of themselves as nurturers, not thinkers. Teachers explained their work in terms of emotional energy, not in terms of thinking. Freeman argues that in connecting teaching with nurturing, many consider teachers' work as a "mindless, low-level skill" (p. 216). In this mind set, teachers are relegated to their classrooms, and others are appointed to make the important decisions related to educational policy.

Yet Head Start staff ultimately interpret and implement policies. It is in the "lived situations of actual teachers—rather than in . . . the educational commissions, policy panels, or research institutions" (Ayers, 1989, p. 4) that policies are interpreted and implemented in daily practice. Staff have always been part of Head Start policy whether or not they are acknowledged.

Although federal review teams monitor grantees every 3 years and require ongoing reporting, and grantees monitor local program staff through periodic on-site inspections and paperwork, local staff operate programs on a daily basis. In an era of Head Start expansion, it is important to understand the processes that staff employ when interpreting official policies in the context of the mundane and extraordinary events that occur in local programs. I sought to understand these processes by examining how the Wood River staff made sense of policies in the daily operation of the program. Four questions provide the framework for my study:

1. How is policy defined in a local Head Start program?
2. How do staff interpret and negotiate official public policies, such as the federal Head Start Performance Standards, licensing regulations for child care centers, and Hoover CAC and Head Start policies?
3. How do local staff negotiate federal and agency policy and local needs?
4. How do staff develop local policies to respond to the ongoing needs and specific problems in the daily operation of the program?

In order to answer these questions I investigated policies from both top-down and bottom-up vantage points.

Vantage Point Analyses

Top-down vantage point interpretation describes how local staff implement official policies. A public policy may be defined as

> an authoritative communication prescribing a course of action for specified categories of individuals in certain anticipated situations. There will be an authority that formulates and enacts the general prescription, agents who refine the prescription and hold people to it, and certain individuals whose action the policy is intended to modify. (Coombs, 1981, p. 53)

At Wood River Head Start, authoritative communications stemmed from three sources: the U.S. Department of Health and Human Services, the state Department of Human Services, and the administrating agency, Hoover Community Action Corporation. Each authoritative communication issued outlines a course of action that explains how objectives will be met and defines those parties responsible for meeting the stated objectives. A time frame for meeting objectives is often specified. Finally, a course of action lists who is to benefit from the stated objectives.

The federal Head Start course of action, aimed at local Head Start grantees, outlines a comprehensive child development program for children whose families' incomes fall below federal poverty guidelines. The state Human Services child care center licensing course of action, aimed at organizations that administer child care programs, specifies minimum standards for equipment, supplies, staff, and facilities for all child care centers. The Hoover CAC's course of action, aimed at specifying how local administrators and program staff provide a comprehensive child development program to young children, delineates staff's responsibilities and local program directives.

Policies define a program and the program's characteristics: the clientele, staffing pattern, and program components. Official policies include courses of action specific enough to give some direction to local staff but broad enough to be subject to multiple local interpretations, because "every policy could be implemented in an infinite number of forms, with each classroom and school creating its own distinctive version of what were intended to be uniform policies" (Pauly, 1991, p. 117). Local program staff interpret and implement official courses of action within the specific context of their specific program: clientele served, length of the program year, and available resources.

This official policy backdrop is present as staff discuss ongoing problems and possible solutions and enact a variety of solutions. Local events, such as eating with the children, counting and recording in-kind donations, supervising the boys' bathroom, riding the bus, and finding out that a child was the victim of a sexual assault, are central to understanding how Head Start staff interpret and implement policies. Program staff "live out" the daily implementation of a Head Start program defined by official policy.

In addition to interpreting and implementing official policies, local staff create policies to cope with ongoing issues such as space allocation, scheduling problems, and crises for individual children and families. Bottom-up vantage point analysis focuses on how staff develop local policies, called policies from practice. Like official policies, policies from practice determine a course of action to guide how staff set up and operate a program. Unlike official policies, policies from practice are developed by the staff themselves and are specific solutions to local problems and change quickly as problems change or are alleviated.

Staff formulate policies from practice based on their working knowledge of official policies, observations of children, and understanding of the relationships among children and staff. The Wood River staff developed policies from practice in response to a complex set of demands: providing comprehensive programs for young children with diverse needs and backgrounds, maintaining indoor and outdoor facilities, responding quickly to emergency situations involving children and families, training new staff members, and reporting attendance and other demographic information to the grantee agency. Staff developed policies from practice to meet the specific needs of the Wood River Head Start community at a specific time.

Wood River has unique characteristics that distinguish it from other Hoover CAC, regional, and national programs. Yet studying the unique events at Wood River can lead to a broader understanding of the social processes operative in other Head Start programs. What connects the unique events at Wood River to events at other Head Start programs are the historical and material forces that shape all events at local sites. Although the same events are enacted differently at other Head Start centers, the types of events are bounded by the general framework of Head Start.

These similarities are understood in the context of local stories. The stories of teachers', parents', and children's daily experiences are key to understanding how policy affects local practice. As Ayers (1989) wrote, "Powerful forces in society have serious and intricate designs on schools . . . any designs must finally be filtered through the minds and hearts and hands of teachers" (p. 5). Staff filter these "designs" in conversation with others and by altering daily practice. The larger social, political, and economic structures, always present, affect how staff filter new designs and envision their implementation.

In examining policy from the perspective of local staff, we might also understand the "taken-for-granted" nature of policy process and that staff's interpretations might lead to different models of policy development and implementation. In this book I use short stories about the mundane and extraordinary events at Wood River to examine how policies are implemented in a program.

CONCLUSION

Head Start policy analysis has relied on large-scale studies that focus on answering two questions: Does Head Start work? What program and curriculum models produce the best results for Head Start children and families? A meta-analysis of Head Start research studies found that children who attend Head Start programs show short-term cognitive and academic gains. Research comparing various Head Start program and curriculum models concluded that different program types can lead to similar outcomes for children and families.

Coupled with recent rapid expansion of Head Start is a concern that programs provide high-quality services to families and children. If the aim is to understand how programs devise and maintain high-quality services, then it is important to study how staff interpret policies and define quality indicators within local programs.

To date, however, Head Start policy research has typically employed an input-output model that assumes a direct link between the intended outcomes of a policy and the implementation of that policy at the local level. These earlier Head Start studies, like most educational policy analysis, is based upon a technical-rational view of knowledge. The premise of technical rationality is that those who systematically study teaching and school systems, rather than those who work in these systems, are best suited to determine educational policy (Schön, 1983, 1987, 1991). From the technical-rational perspective, practitioners are "consumed by the day-to-dayness of school: of finding ways to meet the challenges from one's students, the needs of one's colleagues, the demands of one's supervisors" (Cook, 1994, p. 48), and not by policy making.

The technical-rational perspective does not take into consideration how Head Start staff at various sites interpret and implement policies within the realities of the program. Yet it is precisely this interpretive process that determines how policies are enacted within a particular Head Start program. The paradox in this approach is that it ignores the perspectives of the largely female staff that provide direct services to Head Start children and families.

In shifting policy investigation to local sites, policy "knowledge" is redefined in terms of staff's practices and interpretations. Shifting the grounds of knowing is both an epistemological and political change. In the epistemological sense, it expands policy knowledge to include staff knowledge that has "its roots in a practical knowledge not easily accessible to outsiders, not easily codified and technized" (Ayers, 1989, p. 133). The political change is a shift in recognizing who has knowledge about Head Start policy. This shifting acknowledges that staff at the bottom of the Head Start pyramid are valuable sources from whom to learn about how policy is implemented at local sites. If Head Start staff are active participants in the policy process, then the nature and scope of policy analysis should broaden to include studies of how Head Start staff interpret and implement policies.

Situating policy analysis in stories about a rural Head Start program acknowledges that staff's knowledge about policy may encompass an important source of information about how policies are interpreted and implemented, and also created, at the local level. Moreover, although stories specifically about Wood River are the core of this project, they reflect larger social, economic, and political forces that are always present but often difficult to see. In order to visualize how these forces affect local practice, in the next two chapters I review how Head Start history and organization affects current programs, how various layers of Head Start policy makers and monitors affect local practice, and how changes in the political, economic, and social climate have affected and continue to affect local programs.

2

The Development of Head Start

THE ANGEL ON THE CEILING

If you've traveled to Rome and gone to St. Peter's Basilica, you've seen the work of Michelangelo and the newly restored painting on the Sistine Chapel. There, among the heavenly images, are the child angels, with curly blond hair, serious blue eyes, and pink lips. They are the guardians of the heavenly orbs, everywhere on the edges of celestial events. Their wings are whitish—not golden like those of grown-up counterparts—to reflect their purity and innocence.

I've never made this trip to St. Peter's, but in art classes and on public television I've seen the ceiling and the celestial spirits. I hadn't thought about these angels until I met Brian sitting in circle time, with his long, curly blond hair and large blue eyes, wearing the seriousness of someone pledged to guard the secrets of somewhere, sometime.

"Stand up and tell me about your brothers and sisters," said Judy during circle time.

The children began to stand and rattle off their sibling lists; some needed help remembering names or who their siblings were. Then came Brian's turn. He stood, and in the tone my father used to tell of the day's serious news events, he said with a drawl, "There's Jim an' . . . Chris."

Judy smiled. "Brian has two brothers. Thank you. Sit down now."

And he did, right back in the spot where he had been before. Two nights later he was sitting in a spot between his mother, Katie Lee, and me, eating a banana split. There was chocolate syrup running down his outfit. He'd eaten all the ice cream, but not touched the banana.

"Don't you like bananas?" I asked.

He looked at me, but didn't respond.

"You eat 'em at home," said his mother.

I looked over at her and smiled. She was what some kindly people might call large, and others, less kindly, obese, dressed in old polyester pants and jersey shirt. Her long, reddish hair was parted in the middle, and three of her front teeth were missing. She emitted an odor, unpleasant, yet not overwhelming. We had sat together earlier in the evening for the adult games. She had known the names of all the stars in the game and had won first prize, a Sesame Street plastic character filled with bubble bath. None of the other parents at the table had talked with her.

After the banana splits were eaten, she called to Brian and his brothers, "Time to go," and gathered them up and headed home.

The next day she was back with Brian to help out with the field trip. She came to the boy's bathroom with me. "Smells something awful in here," she complained, and I agreed.

She talked on. "My other boy, Jim, was in Head Start, that was Big River, I couldn't help out then, nobody to watch Brian. Now I've got a good baby-sitter and can come."

For the circle games, Hokey Pokey and Move Like an Animal, she stood beside Brian and did all the motions along with the children and me. At lunch, she giggled when Mark said, "I'm not going to eat anything," and then took one bite of his bread and drank his milk.

"Do they always eat like this?" she asked me.

"Most days," I responded. "Especially Mark."

The next day Brian was back, dressed in a gray jump suit with a motorcycle emblem on the back, "Hey," I called to him, "can I borrow that outfit for tomorrow?"

He smiled, "It's too big for you," he told me.

I offer him my orange corduroy pants and he replied, "I don't wear those sizes."

Brian held my hand as we walked from the restroom to the cafeteria. I recalled holding my own son's hand years ago; he'd had blond curls and blue eyes, too. That day at lunch Brian told me that his father lives in North Dakota. He said, "I don't see him. I live with Mom an' Jim an' baby." Then he ate holes in his slice of bologna and held it up to his face like a mask, saying, "Look at me."

One day, Gale Jolly, the teacher next door, loaned us a guitar she had picked up at a yard sale. It was missing a string and was out of tune. The children vied with one another to have a turn playing it. One day, after waiting patiently, Brian had a turn and climbed into the rocking chair. Rocking back and forth, strumming on the three strings, he sang, "Don' you go breaking my achy breaky heart, achy breaky heart, achy breaky heart. Don' you go breaking my achy breaky heart, my achy breaky heart." For days afterwards, he would take the guitar and sing and rock, sing and rock.

One day in the fall, Judy had the children sitting again and asked them to stand when she called their names and tell her their favorite colors.

"Red," said Brian, and sat down in my lap.

Judy looked at him. "I could just take that one home and keep him." Later that day, I told her how he easily cut the balloon shapes with scissors.

Judy responded, "You know, how does a smart child like that come from a home like that?"

Later that year, Gary complained that Katie Lee wasn't there when they dropped Brian off after school. Ruth, the bus rider, said, "You should just see his face when we pull up and she isn't there." Judy called Katie Lee, and she said she would be there to meet the bus. However, Gary and Ruth continued to report that she often wasn't there. They would then drive around the town until they found someone on Brian's emergency release form, and leave him at that person's house. One day they drove around the small town of Hudson for 15 minutes before they found a place to leave him. Finally, a Head Start social worker went out to talk with Katie Lee. She found Brian's school-age brother, Jim, waiting on the doorstep for his mother. The social worker talked with Jim for a while, and then went home. Later on in the week, she spoke with Katie Lee again about being there when the bus brought Brian home. Katie Lee said she wasn't always sure when the bus would pick up Brian or drop him off.

At home, I would tell my husband and children about Brian. One night I told my husband how Brian had told me he wanted to go to Disneyland. "Oh, Deb," Brian had begun in his drawl, "Mom says Mickey Mouse an' Donald Duck live there. Do they? I have a poster on my wall. You know that's . . . where I want."

As I told the story to John, my voice caught. We'd been making our son's bed, the one who grew out of his blond curls into a preadolescent with body odor and a drum set. Our son who looked so much like this 4-year-old Brian. Our son who, at Brian's age, had already been to Disneyland. John and I walked downstairs, he to listen to a new CD in the living room, me to the basement office and computer, to catch up on my day's field notes. Our children practiced their musical instruments and watched a television show.

The story of Brian and Katie Lee epitomizes the daily lives of many Head Start families, who, in addition to poverty, face other life challenges that hamper them in their efforts to provide experiences similar to those of middle-income families. The formation of Head Start was predicated on the belief that a comprehensive early childhood program would effectively combat the disadvantages of poverty.

Head Start began as a local-federal partnership: The federal government sets program and fiscal standards and provides 80% of the operating budget, and local agencies, called grantees (such as Hoover CAC), operate programs in compliance with federal Performance Standards. Every 4 years, Congress enacts a Head Start bill that authorizes funds for existing programs, delineates new policies, and creates new initiatives. As shown in Figure 2.1, the Head Start Bureau is one of the programs located in the Administration for Children, Youth, and Families in the U.S. Department of Health and Human Services. This department established 10 federal regional offices responsible for monitoring programs within their geographical jurisdiction.

Hoover CAC, located in Region V, is serviced by the regional office in Chicago. Hoover CAC Head Start is assigned to both a program specialist and a fiscal specialist in Chicago. These two individuals are the primary fed-

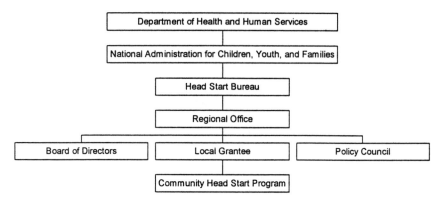

FIGURE 2.1. Head Start Organizational Chart

eral contacts for Hoover CAC Head Start administrators. All fiscal and pro-grammatic reviews of Hoover CAC Head Start emanate from Chicago, and annual and special grant applications are reviewed and approved there.

PLANNING FOR HEAD START

In the late 1950s Americans recognized that the number of people living in poverty was increasing (Harrington, 1962). In 1959, 27% of American fami-lies had incomes below the poverty level (National Research Council, 1976). The rise in poverty rates was due to the decease of available low-skill manu-facturing jobs. The growing civil rights protests alerted middle-class Ameri-cans to the plight of economically disadvantaged minority populations and the reality of riots and civil unrest.

Congress and President Johnson, recognizing Americans' growing con-cerns about poverty and violence, launched the War on Poverty. The Office of Economic Opportunity was developed to administer a wide range of anti-poverty programs (Zigler & Muenchow, 1992; Zigler, Styfco, & Gilman, 1993; Zigler & Valentine, 1979). In 1964 Sargent Shriver, the director of the Office of Economic Opportunity, directed his research division to investigate the national poverty situation. They reported that half of the 30 million people living in poverty were children (Zigler & Muenchow, 1992). The Office of Economic Opportunity, which financed Community Action agencies and other War on Poverty programs, had a budget surplus, and Shriver decided to formulate a new program focusing on children.

Shriver convened a planning committee consisting of doctors, child development specialists, and early childhood educators. This group of 14 devised a working vision for Head Start. The planning committee, spurred on by national support for a new poverty prevention program, reviewed the research on child growth and development and early intervention programs. It was in the context of this national support that the committee interpreted the current social science research (Peters, 1980). In 1964 there were several research projects providing educational services to disadvantaged children. Children enrolled in these programs tested significantly higher after receiving specialized services (Bereiter & Englemann, 1966; Brown, 1978; Gray & Klaus, 1965). Psychologists J. McVicker Hunt (1961) and Benjamin Bloom (1964) focused national attention on the period of early childhood as a time of development critical to later intellectual functioning. Bloom examined the effects of deprivation on children's growth and development. He concluded that high-quality nursery schools could positively influence the intellectual development of culturally deprived children.

The Head Start planning team anticipated that Head Start programs would similarly increase the school performance of children enrolled in the program. Head Start was established on the basis of two assumptions. First, comprehensive early childhood services could positively influence the social competence of young children and low-income children. Second, team members believed that low-income home environments could not provide the stimulation available in those of middle-income families. The committee anticipated that low-income children would benefit greatly from such early childhood services.

Urie Bronfenbrenner, child psychologist and member of the planning team, stated that children are affected by the community. If Head Start was to positively influence young children, the entire community, especially the parents, would have to be involved (Zigler & Muenchow, 1992). The pediatricians on the planning team argued that the program should meet children's basic health and nutritional needs in order for the children to benefit from educational programs. As a result of these recommendations, Head Start was to provide medical, dental, mental health, nutrition, social service, and educational services to all the children enrolled (Biber, 1979; Cohen, Solnit, & Wohlford, 1979; Lazar, 1979; Miller, 1979; North, 1979; Omwake, 1979; Sale, 1979; Stone, 1979). The aim of this comprehensive and community-sensitive approach was to develop socially competent children. Edward Zigler (1979), a member of the Head Start Planning Committee, defines social competence as

> the individual's everyday effectiveness in dealing with his environment. A child's social competence may be described as his ability to master appropriate forms, concepts, to perform well in school, to stay out of trouble with the law, and to relate well to adults and other children. (p. 496)

Martin Deutsch, a member of the planning team and a researcher investigating early intervention programs, recommended that Head Start begin as a pilot project serving 50,000 children. A program of such size would allow researchers to collect data on the children's performance and to begin longitudinal studies of the benefits of Head Start. Deutsch calculated that it would cost $1,000 per child to provide comprehensive services. Shriver argued that the public would not accept a pilot program serving a population of 50,000. Shriver overruled Deutsch's recommendation that Head Start begin as a controlled pilot project and began planning for a large-scale summer program. Head Start budgeted $180 per child for this first program (Zigler & Muenchow, 1992).

Within a year of the first planning meeting, in the summer of 1965, the first Head Start summer session began. The project developed so quickly that it was referred to as Project Rush-Rush (Zigler & Muenchow, 1992). The Office of Economic Opportunity staff sent Head Start proposal applications to community action agencies, school districts, and churches. Staff assisted community groups in completing the required paperwork, locating community facilities, and hiring and training staff. Head Start's first summer program served 561,000 in 2,400 communities at a cost of $96.5 million. The principal grantees were community action agencies and public schools (Collins & Kinney, 1989).

HEAD START BEGINS

The years 1965–1968 mark the first of four stages of Head Start history (Collins & Kinney, 1989). The program served 733,000 children in 1966, 681,400 in 1967, and 693,900 in 1969 (U.S. DHHS, 1997). Most programs operated only during the summer, and due to a lack of adequate facilities and shortages of trained staff, those Head Start programs that were open during the school year often operated for only 4–6 months a year (Datta, 1971; Greenberg, 1990).

Hoover CAC and Wood River Head Start

Hoover CAC began its Head Start operations in 1967 with three summer programs located in two counties that served 127 children at a cost of $25,000. In 1968 Hoover CAC Head Start expanded its summer programs to serve 281 children and added school-year programs in two communities, Arthur and Wood River. Wood River Head Start was located in the basement of St. John's Catholic School and served 16 four-year-old children.

Hope Stand, the first Wood River Head Start teacher, served from 1968 to 1970. Jana Elder, the program aide, recalls that during the first years Head Start was a real "poverty program." The staff had few resources and went from business to business requesting paper and other supplies.

WANING SUPPORT FOR HEAD START

During the second stage of Head Start history, 1969–1972, the overwhelming support that Head Start enjoyed during its first stage waned. Congressional and public support for the War on Poverty was diverted by the war in Vietnam and growing urban violence (Peters, 1980). During this time, the findings of the Westinghouse Study were released. As explained in Chapter 1, the Westinghouse Study found that the cognitive gains of Head Start attendees faded out by the time the children reached third grade. These results, paired with the changing political climate, had a significant impact on Head Start's development. The study challenged the notion that Head Start would eradicate school failure and, subsequently, poverty. Though Head Start was designed as a comprehensive child development program, its success and failure were measured by standardized test scores indicating how Head Start children compared to their non–Head Start peers.

The number of children and families served plummeted during this period. In 1966, during the 2nd year of summer-based programs, Head Start served 733,000 children. In 1971, when most programs had converted from a summer program to a school-year program, the number of children served dropped to 397,000 (U.S. DHHS, 1997). This significant drop in enrolled children was due to the relative cost of serving a child and family in a school-year program compared to the cost of providing a summer program. Because Head Start's budget remained relatively flat from 1969 until 1978 and the cost of providing services increased with inflation, enrollments declined.

Hoover CAC and Wood River Head Start

The Wood River Head Start program had a succession of teachers during this period as they left their Head Start posts when they were offered higher paying public school teaching positions. Typically, Head Start teachers earned wages that qualified them for poverty programs, including medical assistance, food stamps, and fuel assistance.

HEAD START FOCUSES ON IMPROVEMENT

The third stage of Head Start history is referred to as the Edward Zigler period. From 1972 until 1977, under his leadership, Head Start focused on improvement and innovation. These included the creation of the Child Development Associate credential and of the Performance Standards (Collins & Kinney, 1989; Zigler & Muenchow, 1992).

The Child Development Associate (CDA) program is a national credential issued to those individuals who work with preschool children. Candidates in the CDA program attend workshops and classes and prepare a portfolio indicating their competence in 13 areas. Once candidates have completed the certification requirements, they apply to a national council for assessment. The assessment process entails a "written examination, an oral interview, an observation while working with children, questionnaires submitted by parents, and a Candidate portfolio of competency statements and professional resources" (Council for Early Childhood Professional Recognition, 1992, p. 3).

The CDA credential, recognized by Head Start and many state child care center licensing agencies, is not recognized by most public schools as a teaching credential. Thus, CDA certified teachers are limited to Head Start and child care teaching positions that are generally lower paying positions (Collins, 1990; National Head Start, 1990).

The goal of the Performance Standards is to "mandate program quality without being prescriptive in terms of program design" (Washington & Oyemade, 1987). Performance Standards are "the Head Start program functions, activities and facilities required and necessary to meet the objectives and goals of the Head Start program as they relate directly to children and their families" (U.S. DHHS, 1992, p. 1). Health, education, social services, and parent involvement comprise the four major components of the Performance Standards. The Performance Standards are the benchmarks by which all programs are evaluated during federal reviews.

Concurrently, the Head Start Bureau issued new policy directives that included the creation of new training opportunities for Head Start staff, closer monitoring of local Head Start programs, the development and evaluation of different program delivery models that included Parent and Child Centers, Child and Family Resource programs, and Home Start. Parent and Child Centers provided comprehensive services to expectant parents and children aged from birth to 3 years old. Child and Family Resource programs served expectant parents and families with children from birth to 8 years old. The programs provided comprehensive services to families that included early childhood programs for preschool children. Home Start provided Head Start services to young children and their families in their home environment.

Hoover CAC and Wood River Head Start

During this third stage, Hoover CAC Head Start expanded into three additional counties and began offering a home-based program in rural areas. The length of the Hoover CAC Head Start year fluctuated based upon available federal funding. In some years the program year extended into May and in others ended in April.

Wood River Head Start had two different teachers during this time. Emily Short taught from 1972 to 1973 and then, like her predecessors, resigned when offered a full-time public school position. Jana Elder, the program aide since 1968, became the teacher in 1973, after she completed CDA training in Milwaukee. Elder said that Wood River served between 13 and 18 children annually during her teaching tenure. Originally, the program served only 4-year-olds but later expanded service to 3-year-olds. Three-year-olds posed new challenges to the program staff, especially because one staff member had to accompany the children to a second-story bathroom.

Elder recalls how the classroom teacher's paperwork increased during this time. She explained that during her first years at Head Start, teachers only kept track of attendance records and meal counts.

HEAD START EXPANDS

Jimmy Carter's election as president in 1978 marks the beginning of the fourth stage of Head Start history. Congress increased the Head Start budget by a third of the previous funding level, marking the first significant expansion in the program since its inception. The support for expanding Head Start was bipartisan, and funding increases continued under Presidents Reagan, Bush, and Clinton. Head Start entered a period of growth and expansion.

As the funds for Head Start increased, so did the pressure to find indicators that the program was successful. In 1980 President Carter requested that Edward Zigler chair a commission to investigate the present state of the Head Start program and to make recommendations for the program's future. There was a growing concern about the variance in the quality of the existing programs. The commission's recommendations included decreasing class size in compliance with the Head Start Performance Standards, requiring that the teacher in every Head Start classroom obtain a CDA credential, and increasing teacher salaries. Zigler reports that the Reagan administration ignored the commission's recommendations (Zigler & Muenchow, 1992).

The most recently commissioned studies of Head Start are the National Head Start Association's *Report of the Silver Ribbon Panel* (1990) and the Advisory Committee's *Report on Head Start Quality and Expansion* (U.S. DHHS, 1993a). Both studies noted that Head Start provides families and children with comprehensive services and that Head Start programs are generally of high quality. The studies made a number of recommendations for improving the quality of existing programs, providing services to all income eligible families, and creating a new initiative to serve families with infants and toddlers.

In the Head Start Act (1994), signed into law by President Clinton, many of these recommendations were enacted, including

- Allocations for staff salary increases
- Allocations for quality improvement and expansion
- Reorganization and expansion of training and technical assistance
- Requirements for credentialed teaching staff by 1996
- Required federal evaluations of grantees every 3 years
- Allocations for collaboration activities and infant and toddler programs
- Funding for expansion of full-day, full-year programs
- Establishment of a mentor teacher program

President Clinton and his predecessor, President Bush, publicly endorsed expanding Head Start to include all income-eligible children. However, since 1965, Congress has underfunded Head Start (Bolce, 1990; Chafel, 1992a, 1992b; Hymes, 1991; Zigler & Muenchow, 1992; Zigler, Styfco, & Gilman, 1993). Underfunding has resulted in two outcomes. First, the program has not had adequate funding to serve all income-eligible children and families. In 1997, of all the income-eligible families who were qualified for Head Start, 62% of the eligible 4-year-olds and 29% of the eligible 3-year-olds were served at an average cost of $4,571 per child (U.S. DHHS, 1997). Second, current funding levels do not provide funds sufficient for programs to provide high-quality services for families and children. From its inception, Head Start has had a history of inadequate funding for high-quality services. Chafel (1992b) describes the program's inadequate funding:

> According to data provided by the High Scope Educational Research Foundation, per-child funding of Head Start in constant dollars declined by 13% in the eighties, from $3,084 in 1981 to $2,672 in 1989 (Rovner, 1990). By comparison, the Perry Preschool program, often cited as a successful intervention model for disadvantaged children, is funded at a level more than double of Head Start: about $4,963 per child in 1981, which translates to $6,287 in 1989 dollars (Danziger & Stern, 1990).
>
> The low cost per child in the Head Start program is reflected in a number of important indicators of program quality: 1) salaries and benefits, 2) staff training, 3) class size, 4) staffing, and 5) transportation and facilities (Bolce, 1990). (p. 13)

Presidents Bush and Clinton and Congress supported major funding increases for Head Start, and the budget doubled between 1991 and 1997, as

TABLE 2.1. Federal Funding for Head Start

Fiscal Year	Billions of Dollars
1991	1.95
1992	2.20
1993	2.78
1994	3.25
1995	3.53
1996	3.57
1997	3.98

Source: U.S. DHHS, 1997, pp.1-2.

depicted in Table 2.1. However, as in the past, the actual funds allocated for Head Start have fallen short of proposed presidential and congressional committee budgets. For instance, the projected budget for FY 1994 was "authorized to reach $7.6 billion" (Meadows, 1991, p. 9), but, as noted in Table 2.1, the actual amount allocated was just over $3.2 billion.

Hoover CAC and Wood River Head Start

During the 1984–85 school year, Hoover CAC Head Start added home-based and center-based services to three additional counties. Funded enrollment increased in 1984–85 from 155 to 207 children. In 1987, the state legislature appropriated state funds for Head Start, and with these funds, Hoover CAC expanded services to an additional 55 families. Utilizing federal and state funding increases in 1990, the program expanded again to serve an additional 49 children.

At the Wood River program, Jana Elder taught until 1983, when she "got canned." She recalls that a program administrator, inspecting the program, said that she was "hollering at the kids." Elder stated that she could have protested her dismissal, but decided not to. Luci Quist, Elder's aide, became the Wood River teacher. Subsequently, Judy Roberts, Quist's aide, became the Wood River teacher in 1991.

SUMMARY

Social, political, and economic trends have affected Head Start history. The program began in 1965 as part of the War on Poverty, and as national attention shifted to the war in Vietnam, support for the program waned. From

1970 to 1980, Head Start continued to operate but served fewer children than it had in 1965. Under the direction of Edward Zigler, the Head Start Bureau developed policies to monitor program quality and enhance staff qualifications. From 1980 until the present, public support for Head Start has grown, and funding levels have increased significantly.

The history of the Hoover CAC and Wood River Head Start reflects the development of the national program. The first programs operated only during the summer months. During the 1970s, program resources were limited, and staff relied upon local business donations to supplement classroom materials. Wood River teachers often left their positions to teach in elementary schools. Three of the Wood River program aides became teachers after completing the Child Development Associate credential program.

Hoover CAC, like other Head Start grantees, is responsible for operating programs in compliance with federal policies. It is the Hoover CAC Head Start administrative staff that monitors local program staff to determine if programs are in compliance with federal and agency standards. In the next chapter, I describe the organization of Hoover CAC and Head Start administrative staff, and that of the Wood River staff.

3

Looking at the Hoover Community Action Corporation and Wood River Head Start

---

NO BOOZE, NO CIGGIE TEE SHIRTS

During my second week at Wood River we were going to an apple orchard for a field trip. Judy, Susan, and I were sitting in the gym eating bagels and cream cheese with the children who arrived on the first bus route.

Judy turned to me and said, "I forgot to tell you. You could wear jeans today. It's always okay to wear black or white jeans but blue jeans only on field trip days."

"Why's that?" I asked.

Susan explained, "It's the dress code here, no blue jeans for anyone, not even the bus driver or aide. You can't wear those pants for running either, anything with elastic around the ankle."

"But stirrups?" I asked.

Judy answered, "Those are okay, I wear them all the time, the other thing is you can't wear booze or ciggie tee shirts."

I laughed, but neither Susan or Judy joined in.

Judy continued, "Yeah, none of those booze or ciggie tee shirts, or sweatshirts, you can't wear 'em here."

I later learned that the Hoover CAC director had developed the dress code policy in response to a concern that some office staff dressed inappropriately for work. When the dress code policy was developed it was applied to all Hoover CAC staff, including Head Start personnel. This story about booze and ciggie tee shirts highlights how the administrative structure and organization of grantees affects how local programs operate. Grantees supervise and evaluate program staff, require documentation of daily activities, equipment, and food service, and devise and enforce policies specifically for employees. In the same sense that federal Head Start history helps explain how local programs operate, grantee structure and organization illuminate how local programs function.

HOOVER CAC HEAD START

When I began my study in 1993, Hoover CAC operated 15 center-based and 11 home-based Head Start programs that served nearly 400 young, economically impoverished children and their families. Head Start employed 9 administrators and office staff, 25 center- and home-based teachers, 38 assistant teachers and site aides, 12 bus drivers and riders, and 4 family advocates. Head Start staff, like other personnel who worked in other Hoover CAC programs, are Hoover CAC employees. Hoover CAC determines personnel policies, salary schedules, and grievance procedures.

In addition to managing Head Start, Hoover CAC operated 19 health, educational, and human services programs, including weatherization, senior dining, and social services, in six counties. In 1992, $1.3 million of the Hoover CAC $7.8 million budget was allocated to Head Start (Hoover CAC, 1992a). Only the energy assistance program, with an annual budget of $2.5 million, exceeded Head Start's expenditures. The area encompasses Agel, the site of a 2-year-long meat packers strike; Barrymore, home to migrant farmworkers; Wering, a river town; Camden, the wild-turkey capital of the state; and Harvard, home to conservative Amish who refuse to use slow-moving vehicle signs. From the banks of the rivers to the plains, this is corn, soy bean, and dairy-farm country. The plains land is rich and productive, and generations of Scandinavian and German farmers have worked the family farms. Travel in the country is limited to two-lane roads. The land is logged as well; the logging trails snake up and down the hills along the Wood River. The median family income in 1986 for this area ranged from a high of $26,410 to a low of $19,108 (Hoover CAC, 1989). Approximately 8,020 of the 36,655 children under 8 live in families with annual incomes below $20,000 (Hoover CAC, 1989).

There are two Hoover CAC Head Start policy-making boards that determine the policies for Head Start programs such as Wood River. The first is the Hoover CAC Head Start Policy Council. The council is composed of parents with children enrolled in a Head Start program, parents whose children previously attended a Head Start program, and community representatives. Head Start Performance Standards require that programs set up policy councils. The councils reflect the program's philosophy of including "parents as partners" to accomplish program goals. Each Hoover CAC home- and center-based program elects one policy council delegate. The policy council approves all Head Start policies, staff changes, program expansion, and grant proposals.

The second board that determines Head Start operations is the Hoover CAC Board of Directors. This board is composed of community representatives from the six county service area and is responsible for reviewing and approving all agency policies, grant proposals, salary increases, and procedural and staff changes.

In 1990 the Hoover CAC Head Start Policy Council and Hoover CAC Board of Directors approved the Hoover CAC Head Start *Policies and Procedures Manual.* This manual consists of 15 parts: Hoover CAC agency information, Hoover CAC personnel rules and regulations, the state Department of Human Services Child Care Center Licensing Regulations, Performance Standards, job descriptions, and information concerning center- and home-based education programs, health services, parent involvement, recruitment, social service, special needs, transportation, volunteers, and staff. Each center- and home-based program received a copy of the manual. It describes the organizational structure of center-based programs and the roles and responsibilities of each Head Start center-based staff member.

Ann Norstrom, as the Hoover CAC Head Start director, oversaw all Hoover CAC Head Start administrative staff. She reported to the Hoover CAC executive director and developed annual budgets that the Hoover CAC Head Start Policy Council and Hoover CAC Board of Directors reviewed and approved.

The other Hoover CAC Head Start supervisory staff comprised managers and county coordinators. County coordinators were responsible for supervising programs within a certain geographical area. For instance, Martha Calle, the coordinator for Wood River, oversaw Head Start programs in two counties, supervising and evaluating all home- and center-based staff in her assigned region. Managers supervised a particular component of the Head Start program. The health manager inspected the kitchen facilities, conducted hearing tests at programs, and kept track of all children's and staff's health records. The transportation manager, in addition to the county coordinator, supervised and evaluated bus drivers. The social service manager supervised all social service staff, referred to as family advocates. The parent involvement component manager supervised all parent-related activities, including parent meetings, newsletters, and volunteering. At Hoover CAC, several administrators were both county coordinators and component managers. For instance, Martha Calle was the Wood River county coordinator and the special needs component manager. Martha was responsible for monitoring services to young children with disabilities at all center- and home-based programs. Head Start since the 1970s has mandated that 10% of the children served be children with disabilities.

Hoover CAC Head Start administrators monitored local programs through direct and indirect means. Direct monitoring occurred when administrators inspected the program and evaluated the staff's performance. The county coordinator visited each program a minimum of three times and wrote up an evaluation of each visit. The health manager inspected the kitchen, meal procedures, and children's health records twice during the 1993–94 year. In this period, the program dietitian inspected the kitchen and meal procedures twice, and the transportation manager evaluated bus procedures once.

Indirect monitoring included paperwork and phone calls through which to report program changes to Hoover CAC. Each week Head Start program staff submitted to Hoover CAC lesson plans, site inspection forms, and accident reports. On a monthly basis staff submitted medication log forms, family case history notes, in-kind donation summary forms, parent meeting minutes and attendance forms, volunteer forms, a monthly parent newsletter, attendance record, meal count form, field trip forms, driver's bus inspection form, and a bus mileage and service record form. At Wood River, Judy and Susan spent the last day of month completing forms that they sent to the office. Hoover CAC required programs to inform the office of any upcoming changes in the regular schedule, including field trips, menu changes, and staff absences. Staff were required to report cases of suspected child abuse and neglect and that of any child with three or more unexcused absences. Program staff called Hoover CAC to request supplies, clarify policies and procedures, report problems, and inform staff of programmatic changes.

WOOD RIVER HEAD START

Established 25 years ago, Wood River Head Start is one of the four oldest center-based Hoover CAC programs. Until 1993, the program was located in rented classroom space in the basement of St. John's Catholic Church, and the staff consisted of a classroom teacher, assistant teacher or teacher aide, bus driver, and site aide. The teacher was responsible for setting up and running the preschool program, conducting two home visits to each family, and supervising center staff. An assistant teacher, who was teacher certified, or a teacher aide, who met agency and state child care licensing qualifications, assisted the teacher in setting up activities, organizing materials, and cleaning. The bus driver drove the bus on morning and afternoon routes and maintained the vehicle. The site aide rode the bus with the driver, prepared meals, and cleaned the kitchen and eating areas.

The staff provided three and a half hours of preschool Monday through Thursday from mid-September through early May to eighteen 3- and 4-year-old children and their families. The children were divided into two bus routes to comply with a Hoover CAC policy stating that children could not ride the bus for more than one hour per route. One group of children arrived at 9:00 A.M. and another group arrived at 10:00 A.M. The staff fed the children snack at 10 and then provided them with an array of preschool activities that included art, music, gym time, storytelling, and play time. After the children ate lunch at noon, the group of children who arrived at 9:00 A.M. departed, at 12:30 P.M. The second group of children left for home at 1:30 P.M.

Teaching staff were contracted for 32 hours weekly to provide 18 hours of preschool, supervise staff, and complete lesson plans and paperwork. Assistant teachers, bus drivers, and site aides were contracted for the specific hours in which they would provide direct service to families and children.

The members of the four-person Wood River Head Start staff were mentioned in the opening story of the book, but now I want to introduce them in more depth.

Judy Roberts

Judy Roberts, a slim and attractive person, told me several times that she "loved her job" as a Head Start teacher. Judy, her husband, Tom, and her two sons lived in Drake, a river town located 12 miles from the Wood River Head Start program. Judy had a large number of siblings living in the area and often spent weekends on family outings. She and her husband enjoyed traveling, and during my first year at Wood River she took two one-week vacations with Tom and also attended the National Head Start Association Training Conference in Kentucky.

Judy first began her involvement in Head Start as a parent volunteer when her sons attended the program. She was then offered the job as the aide in the Wood River program, and after receiving her CDA certificate, became first the assistant teacher and then the teacher at Wood River. She told me that during her years as an aide and assistant teacher she was "doing all the cleanup. I didn't get to do anything with the children. The teacher did all of that. So when she was gone, and I had to teach, I didn't know what to do. I didn't know how to read a book or anything."

Judy described her transition from assistant teacher to teacher as difficult: "I had to learn how to do everything on my own. It was like starting out as a brand-new teacher." Judy talks about how much she has grown over the past 8 years in her role as the Wood River teacher. Kathryn Shay, a parent of a former Head Start child who participated with me in renewing Judy's CDA credential, commented to Judy on "how much more comfortable you seem. It used to be when people asked you questions, you would get all flustered. Now you seem to know how to handle things, and it goes better."

Hoover CAC recently moved to a site-based management model for center-based programs. Each Head Start center-based program has a site manager, who is usually the classroom teacher. In her dual roles as classroom teacher and site manager, Judy plans the children's daily activities and completes the paperwork required by Hoover CAC, supervises and evaluates the

Wood River staff, orders supplies and equipment, updates children's files, arranges and runs staff meetings, and reports changes in schedule and emergencies to Hoover CAC. Hoover CAC and child care licensing regulations require that programs maintain up-to-date records on children, fire drills, meal counts, lesson plans, accident reports, case notes on individual children, volunteer logs, attendance, and in-kind donations. Judy submits weekly and monthly paperwork to the Hoover CAC.

Susan Jensen

Susan Jensen, a relative newcomer to Wood River, was beginning her second full year as the assistant teacher in 1993. Though to me she appeared very competent, she told me that her initial transition from day care to Head Start had been difficult. She explained that it took her "a long time to figure out what to do, because nobody told me." Susan, the only blonde staff member, reflected the Scandinavian heritage of the area. Her long hair, blue eyes, and quiet composure are characteristic of many of its residents. Susan enjoyed arts-and-crafts projects and was often working on a gift for a relative or friend. She extended her talents to Head Start and created flannel-board story characters, bulletin boards, and pleasing visual displays for the classroom.

Susan had graduated from nearby Blue River State College with a bachelor's degree in elementary education and had a current elementary teaching license with a kindergarten endorsement. When teaching vacancies occurred in public and private elementary schools, Susan applied for the positions. She told me that it is difficult to get a teaching job in this area and that her local superintendent prefers not to hire teachers who had graduated from the local high school.

At Wood River, Susan was offered, and accepted, the position of assistant teacher. This rank indicated that she was teacher qualified. When Judy was sick or requested vacation time, Susan was able to substitute for her, with a substitute found, in turn, to assist Susan.

Susan is married and lives with her farming husband, Joel, in Carleton, a community 11 miles from Wood River. Unlike in the case of Judy and Ruth, who both described their pay as supplemental to that of their husbands', Susan's Head Start salary provides the mainstay of her family's income. To supplement this income, Susan also worked for another Hoover CAC Head Start home-based program every other Friday; at the local drug store as a data entry clerk; for the local school district as the assistant coach for girls' gymnastics; and as the teacher for Carleton's summer recreation program. Though Susan, like other Hoover CAC Head Start staff, could apply for and receive unemployment benefits during the summer months, she chose instead to work in the drug store and the recreation program. She told me she would prefer to work than collect unemployment benefits.

Ruth Donalds and Gary Nielson

Ruth Donalds, like me, was a newcomer to Wood River Head Start. She had recently moved to Starr with her husband and two children. Her husband, Ron, had an administrative job with a railroad company. Ruth had worked previously with children but never with a Head Start program. Ruth is an attractive, slim brunette, a devoted mother, and a volunteer in many of her children's activities. She quickly became a favorite of the Head Start children. She has a calm and kind but firm nature that signals to children that she is genuinely interested in their well-being and safety.

Ruth's major responsibilities included riding the bus for two one-hour morning and afternoon routes, serving lunch, washing dishes, and cleaning the kitchen and lunch room. Ruth told me that one thing that was different about working for Head Start was the number of meetings and training sessions she was required to attend.

Gary Nielson was the Head Start bus driver. He and his wife, long-time residents of Starr, frequently visited his nearby adult children and grandchildren. Gary had served in the navy in a bomber squadron in World War II and had retired from his previous position as a marketing representative for an oil and gasoline company. He has a commercial driver's license that certifies him to drive school buses. In addition to working for Hoover CAC, Gary worked for a bus company on Fridays, weekends, and during the summer months, driving school groups to field trips and senior citizen groups on sight-seeing tours.

In 1993 Gary began his 6th year of Head Start bus driving. Gary's responsibilities include driving four daily bus routes, transporting the Head Start lunch, keeping daily mileage and fuel records, and fueling and maintaining the bus.

In August 1993, Ruth and Gary joined the other staff as they packed and moved the Head Start program from St. John's Catholic School to the Wood River Early Learning Center. This move was spurred by the latest federal review.

THE FEDERAL INSPECTION OF WOOD RIVER

Every 3 years a federal review team inspects the administrative and programmatic aspects of a Head Start agency's program operations. The team uses the on-site program review instrument, a 123-page checklist comprising 256 items divided into eleven sections: education, health, mental health, nutrition, social services, parent involvement, disabilities services, eligibility and recruitment, administration, options, and financial/property management.

During an on-site review, team members examine program records and fiscal procedures and visit several program sites. During the site visits, the team members complete the On-Site Program Review Instrument checklists, indicating whether the program is in compliance with federal standards. Team members conduct interviews, complete observations, and inspect program records to complete the checklists.

At the end of an on-site review visit, the federal team meets with the agency's administrative staff and reviews the team's findings. The team then submits a written report to the agency and federal office. When a program is found to be out of compliance with certain standards, the Head Start administrative agency must respond to the report with a written plan of action to remedy the noncompliance citations.

One member of the federal team who visited the Wood River site decided that the facility was not adequate and noted in a report that the center was out of compliance with federal standards. Of particular concern was the lack of hot water in the building, both in the bathrooms and classrooms, and the poor hall lighting.

Ann Norstrom, the Head Start director, decided to find a new location for the program. She then began negotiations with the local public school. She hoped that their Early Learning Center, located in Wood River and housing kindergarten and early childhood programs, would provide the needed space for the Head Start program.

UNDERSTANDING THE CONTEXT OF HEAD START

The move from St. John's to the Early Learning Center exemplifies how local Head Start programs are nested in various contexts (see Figure 3.1).

Three contexts—the American social, economic, and political climate; the federal framework as delineated by legislation, policies, and budget allocations; and the grantee's organization, policies, and monitoring of local program staff—shape the organization and operation of local programs.

Head Start, unlike most War on Poverty programs, survived the shift in national agenda toward the war in Vietnam. One reason that Head Start may have survived is that part of the American social agenda is to provide basic services—health and dental care, nutrition, and education—to all children, including children living in poverty. The goal of Head Start, states Peters (1980), "was construed as part of a national attack on a highly visible societal crisis—one involving poverty and inequality of opportunity" (p. 24).

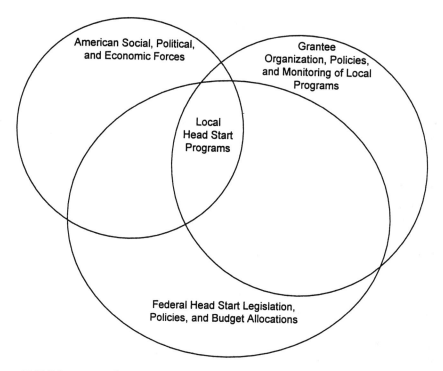

FIGURE 3.1. Local Program Context

However, budget allocations for Head Start have never been adequate to serve all income-eligible 3- and 4-year-olds, expand services to children under 3 years of age, or fund the program at levels comparable to other early intervention programs that document both short- and long-term benefits for children. As a result of underfunding, Head Start staff salaries are generally lower than those of other publicly funded early childhood positions, and as in the case of Wood River, certified teachers often leave their positions with Head Start for higher paying jobs in public schools.

When Head Start first began, there were few rules governing program operation. Historically, the regulatory structure of federal programs such as Head Start has been weak, and the local administrative agencies, such as Hoover CAC, are quite autonomous (Cohen & Spillane, 1992). The federal response to this loose structure is to impose more and more rules and regulations upon local agencies. In the mid-1970s, under the direction of Edward Zigler, the Head Start Bureau issued the Head Start Performance Standards, new qualifications for teaching staff, and policies designed to upgrade the quality of Head Start programs and monitor the activities of grantees. Hoover CAC, like other grantees, is subject to a "vast regulatory enterprise" (Timar, 1994, p. 53). As this enterprise grew, "rules became increasingly narrow and prescriptive" (p. 5). In response to the increase in federal rules and policies, grantees focused more and more on documentation and rule compliance.

At both the federal and grantee level, a Head Start administrative structure was established that focused on monitoring and compliance. When federal reviews are conducted, every 3 years, team members interpret how well programs implement and comply with federal policies. These interpretations have significant consequences for local programs, as exemplified by the report that St. John's School was not in compliance with federal standards. This report prompted the move from St. John's to the Early Learning Center.

At the grantee level, complying with the myriad of federal and state child care licensing regulations entails both direct and indirect monitoring of local staff. Pressed to document program operations, Head Start administrators require local staff to complete detailed records of daily operations covering all aspects of the program. At Hoover CAC Head Start, each week teaching staff have nearly the same amount of time scheduled for planning, paperwork, and home visiting as they have for implementing the preschool program.

In the present climate of burgeoning Head Start policies, teachers and administrators are faced with increasing numbers of mandates and regulations. How staff make sense of these policies and regulations is a critical factor in how policy is implemented and the quality of services provided to children and families. Local policy meanings are formulated at the intersection of local stories, staff biographies, local program history, and more global frameworks, including economic, political, and social forces, Head Start organizational patterns, and federal and grantee policies and histories.

In Part II, I present short stories about the daily and extraordinary events at Wood River. The stories are not mirror images of the activities and conversations that occurred at Wood River, but rather an account (Richardson, 1995), based upon my lived experience with the Wood River staff and children.

I chose storied text for four reasons. First, narratives, such as short stories, are commonly used to describe events. As Bruner (1990) writes:

> [I]n understanding cultural phenomena, people do not deal with the world event by event or with text sentence by sentence. They frame events and sentences in larger structures. . . . These larger structures provide an interpretive context for the components they encompass. (p. 64)

When Wood River Head Start staff talked about policy, they framed this talk in a larger story narrative: They talked about how policy "fit into" a particular story.

Second, the stories draw readers into the everyday world at Wood River Head Start:

> In telling a story, the author attempts to weave a text that re-creates for the reader the real world that was studied. Subjects, including their actions, experiences, words, intentions, and meanings, are then anchored inside this world as the author presents experience-near, experience-distant, local, and scientific theories of it. Readers take hold of this text and read their way into it, perhaps making it one of the stories they will tell about themselves. They develop their own naturalistic generalizations and impressions, based on the tacit knowledge and emotional feelings the text creates for them. (Denzin, 1994, p. 507)

The stories I wrote about Wood River, through their descriptions and narrative structure, invite readers into the worlds described.

Third, stories contexualize Head Start policies "in a particular spatial and temporal site, a particular configuration of the everyday/everynight world" (Smith, 1990, p. 91). Policies, although seemingly invisible, formed the underlying structure of the program and are manifest in the staff's stories. Wood River staff took policies for granted and only talked about them as they related to particular troubles at the program. Yet policies determined who worked at Wood River, how the program operated, the program's clientele, and administrative structure. These policies, or texts, mediate how staff organize and operate the program (D. Smith, 1992).

Finally, stories provide a conduit to the larger cultural-historical context. "These stories should be connected to larger institutional, group, and cultural contexts, including written texts and other systems of discourse" (Denzin, 1994, p. 511). Stories are both descriptions of unique events and exemplars of historical trends, and political, cultural and economic forces.

Through the stories I aim to describe how policy is interwoven into the daily activities at the program, not confined to isolated conversations among the staff or program administrators. The stories invite readers, through my experiences, to enter the world of Wood River as I knew it, seeing, hearing, and feeling (Wolcott, 1990). The connecting text between the stories explains how the Wood River staff and I interpreted policies related to the stories' events.

PART II

Windows on Policy

4

The Move to the Early Learning Center

A HOT SULTRY DAY IN AUGUST

It was a humid August day when we moved the Wood River Head Start program out of the basement of St. John's Catholic School. I had called ahead and asked Judy if she would like some help. "Sure, come whenever you'd like," she told me. I drove up early that morning with my children, and we helped pack boxes and stack them into the U-Haul. Gary, the bus driver, and Ruth, the site aide, made two trips to the rented storage unit, 11 miles away.

As we carried out boxes, sweat pouring down our faces, the St. John's kindergarten teacher, principal, and parent volunteers began painting the walls and woodwork. The rooms would once again house the St. John's kindergarten program. We carried out loads of materials to the trash area. "I just don't have any place to keep this," complained Judy. We filled the large dumpster and many boxes with trash.

Judy looked at the two adjoining rooms at St. John's. She compared the spacious accommodations to the small room she was to share with the family education program at the local public school. The rooms at St. John's were large and provided ample space for a well-equipped early childhood classroom, including a kitchen area, blocks, books, a large carpeted area for story and circle time, a storage area, and a space for staff's and children's belongings. Gary and Ruth moved most of the play equipment from these large rooms to the storage unit. There was no room for it in the shared class-room. When we arrived at the public school, the janitors were waxing the floors, and we had to pile things in the corner. Judy and Susan, the assistant teacher, waited several days before they were able to get into the room to arrange the shelves and unpack the supplies.

Two weeks later, I was conducting a training session for 100 Hoover CAC staff from 15 center-based and 11 home-based programs. The training was attended by teachers, assistant teachers, aides, and bus drivers and was part of an annual in-service training program. The topic of the training was how adults can help children learn new skills. During lunch, I sat with Judy and decided that this would be a good time to ask her when I could start volunteering with the program.

Judy looked down and said, "Give us a few days to get started." Then she added, "At least one. What if you start on Tuesday? You know how hard it is at the start." Wood River would begin a week after Labor Day. I could remember from my own days of teaching that at the start of the year, the first order of business was for me to get to know the children.

I told her that was fine, and I waited for Tuesday to come. I wondered if Judy really wanted me to come at all. The first thing she said when I got in the door on Tuesday was, "Well, I guess you should have come yesterday. We could have really used you then!"

The reason that Judy said she could have used me was that the child care licensing agent from the state Department of Human Services came unannounced during the first day to inspect and license the facility as a child care center. Wood River, like all other Head Start programs, is required to obtain state licensing as a child care facility. Licensing requirements vary state to state but generally involve an on-site inspection of the facility, children's records, and staff qualifications.

Apparently, Hoover CAC had been informed of the visit, but the message never reached Judy. She and Susan had just begun their first day of Head Start, with an open house for parents and children to come and visit, when the child care agent arrived. Judy spent the morning showing the agent the necessary files, paperwork, and facility. The agent told Judy that the room was not large enough to accommodate the 18 children that Hoover CAC Head Start classrooms usually enroll. Classroom capacity for child care facilities is determined by square footage, and the room was only big enough to accommodate 16 children. Despite the inadequacy of the room size, the agent licensed the facility for 17 children.

Luckily, at the beginning of the year there were only 14 children enrolled. Several parents had to withdraw their children due to transportation and work-related problems. The vacant slots filled eventually, but not for a few weeks.

On my first day at Head Start, I noticed a picture from the September edition of the *Starr–Wood River School Update* newsletter hanging on the bulletin board outside the kitchen doorway. In the center of the picture sat Judy and Fran Mark, the family education coordinator, looking at a book. Standing behind Fran was Gale Jolly, the special education teacher. Susan stood near Judy, looking down at the book. Gale and Fran were smiling in the picture, though Judy and Susan looked solemn. The caption under the picture read:

Head Start, Family Education and Special Education staff members
got together recently to plan the shared space for the three Early Child-

hood programs. The three programs will be located in the lower level of the Early Learning Center beginning this fall.

What stayed with me over the first weeks of fall was the contrast of the pictured calmness of Judy and Susan and the daily problems they encountered in negotiating the shared space.

RELOCATING HEAD START

Wood River Head Start had always been the program in St. John's basement. When people asked about Head Start, they were directed to St. John's. The Head Start rooms were full of momentos from the earliest days at the program, including pictures for bulletin boards, toys in need of repair, and a full array of preschool equipment and supplies. Judy's sons, one a high school graduate and the other a high school junior, had attended Head Start at St. John's. When Judy first heard that her program would need to relocate, she asked Ann Norstrom to request a variance for a year. During that period Hoover CAC could apply for federal funds for a mobile unit. Federal regulations prohibited Hoover CAC from purchasing permanent Head Start facilities with federal funds, though specified federal funding was available for portable classroom units. Once Hoover CAC received the funds and the portable unit was constructed, the program could move into its new facility. Ann, while agreeing to apply for funds for the mobile unit, decided that the program would move immediately to a new facility.

There are three reasons that Ann decided to relocate the program immediately. First, the federal team insisted that the Wood River program be relocated. Second, when Martha Calle, the Wood River county supervisor, called St. John's and spoke with the priest about moving the program, he indicated that the church had plans to use the space to house a kindergarten program. Third, Ann, like other Head Start directors, responded to the federal mandate requiring agencies to collaborate with other early childhood programs by collocating Head Start with other early childhood programs.

Collocation refers to the practice of placing Head Start programs in the same location as other programs (Guralnik, 1980). The aim is to enhance program collaboration, the practice of programs working together to provide services. There is a national Head Start initiative for collaboration with state and local programs. Under Ann's direction, Hoover CAC Head Start programs were collocated with other early childhood programs, such as the Wood River Early Learning Center.

The Early Learning Center Programs

Originally the building to which Head Start moved housed the Wood River Elementary School. When the Wood River and Starr school districts consolidated, the Wood River Elementary School became the Early Learning Center. In 1993 the Early Learning Center housed three different public school programs: 3 kindergarten classes, the special education program, and the family education program.

The kindergarten program occupied the upper story of the building and consisted of three spacious classrooms, a playroom equipped with learning centers, boys' and girls' bathrooms, storeroom, and staff bathroom. The school district bused children from Starr and Wood River for a half-day kindergarten program, which was staffed by three kindergarten teachers.

The special education and family education programs, like the kindergarten programs, are administered by the Starr–Wood River school district. The special education program serves children from birth through age 5 who qualify for special education services. Each spring the school district invites all 3-year-olds to preschool screening to identify children who, after undergoing a full assessment, may qualify for special education services. Each child who thus qualifies has an individualized educational plan that delineates which types of services the child will receive. Individual plans might include speech, occupational, or physical therapy and either home or center-based educational services. The center-based special education program is a half-day program operating Monday, Tuesday, Thursday, and Friday and consists of a preschool curriculum, occupational, physical, and speech therapy, and an adaptive physical education class. The program staff included Gale Jolly, the teacher; two program aides; and speech, occupational, and physical therapy specialists. Gale Jolly began the special education program 13 years ago.

The family education program serves expectant parents and families with children from birth to 5. The program is open to all families residing in the district and consists of home visits and center-based parent education and early childhood classes. A typical center-based family education class consists of a 2-hour session. During the first half hour, parents and children work on a project (art activity, science experiments, woodworking or storytelling). Then the children remain in the classroom with an early childhood teacher while the parents leave for an hour-long parent education session. Following the session, parents and children select toys, books, and learning materials from the lending library. Family education programs are offered during the morning, afternoon, and evening hours. The family education staff were Fran Mark, the program coordinator and parent educator; an early childhood teacher; and a program aide.

Wood River Head Start, special education, and family education programs sometimes served the same children and families. For instance, families with incomes below poverty level who were enrolled in Head Start would receive special education services if their preschool child met the special education criteria. In these cases, children were dually enrolled in Head Start and special education services. The special education staff provides additional services, based upon the child's individual educational plan, during the scheduled Head Start day. All Head Start families living within the school boundaries could enroll in family education classes. During the year, some Head Start parents enrolled their children in a school readiness classes scheduled prior to or after a Head Start session.

Negotiating Space for Head Start

During an initial meeting between Hoover CAC Head Start administrators and Early Learning Center staff, the kindergarten teachers made it clear that their second-story space was off-limits to Head Start. When Hoover CAC Head Start administrators suggested that the Head Start children use the kindergarten playroom from 10:00 A.M. until 11:00 A.M., the kindergarten teachers responded with the comment that "Head Start children are too young to use those materials."

In a subsequent meeting with Martha Calle, the Hoover CAC Head Start Wood River County Coordinator, Judy, Susan, and the Early Learning Center staff, it was decided that Head Start would be located exclusively on the first floor. This floor contained two classrooms, boys' and girls' rest rooms, the kitchen, and gym. The special education program used one of the classrooms and the family education program the other. Fran Mark, the family education teacher, originally said that her program's classroom could accommodate Head Start's 9:00 A.M. to 2:00 P.M. schedule, but in a later meeting she stated that the family education program would need the room until 11:00 A.M., 3 days per week.

Following these negotiations, Ann worked out an agreement with the school district superintendent that the Head Start program would use the room shared with the family education program from 11:00 A.M. to 2:30 P.M. As required by Hoover CAC regulations limiting bus routes to one-hour runs, Head Start children would arrive in two groups. Children from Starr and the surrounding communities would arrive at 10:00 A.M. and carry out activities in the gym until 11:00 A.M. The special education program would also use the gym from 10:00 A.M. until 11:00 A.M. daily. The superintendent agreed to install a divider to separate the gym into one area for the Head Start program and another for the special education program. Head Start agreed to pay for the installation of the divider. There would also be a storage area constructed in the teachers' lounge for Head Start and the family education program. In August, the Wood River school board approved this rental agreement.

Judy and Fran Mark, the family education coordinator, met and decided what to put in the shared room. The room, with windows and fluorescent lighting, was well lit. There was a sink in the room and an adjoining bathroom. Part of the floor was carpeted and the rest tiled. Judy selected some of the Head Start housekeeping equipment, toys, puzzles, and supplies for the room, and Fran added toys and learning games, shelving, tables, and chairs.

After Judy and Fran arranged the materials, the room contained a play kitchen area, wooden and cardboard brick blocks, books, puzzles, Fisher Price play sets, and a variety of games and small cars and trucks. There was a file cabinet for Head Start files and a storage cupboard for arts and crafts supplies. There were three child-sized tables and chairs to accommodate the children for arts activities.

THE DAILINESS OF WOOD RIVER HEAD START

As a result of the agreement that Ann negotiated with the school district superintendent, Judy had to rearrange the Head Start schedule around that of the other Early Learning Center programs. On September 27, she posted the daily schedule (see Figure 4.1).

Susan and Judy worked before school to prepare the activities for the children. This included gathering the supplies for the morning activities and carrying them from the shared classroom to the gym, preparing snack, and planning lessons. In addition, they had to complete the required Head Start paperwork and photocopy handouts and parent newsletters. At the start of the year, the paperwork took considerable time. Judy commented to me at the end of the 2nd week, "There is so much paperwork to do, I have hardly had any time to be with the kids."

Lesson Planning

Hoover CAC required Head Start staff to develop and submit daily lesson plans incorporating curriculum themes developed by Hoover CAC. These themes were developed by the home- and center-based education and health component managers in response to two findings of the 1989 federal review team. The first was that the program did not have a standard curriculum. The federal education team member stated that Hoover CAC could either purchase one or develop its own curriculum. Second, the health team member found that mandated health and safety topics were not addressed in the center-based schedule. These included fire and tornado drills and health pro-

10:00	First group arrives; children hang their coats in the hallway. Judy and Susan arrive at 8:00 and get materials ready. Susan makes snack for first group. Gary picks Ruth up at 9:00 and begins bus route through Starr and Wood River; they return with first group at 10:00.
10:05–10:40	Staff check children's backpacks for notes and supervise children in the bathrooms. Snack and washing (rest rooms located in the hallway, snack in the gym). Art project in gym following snack. Gary and Ruth pick children up in Hudson.
10:40–11:00	Gym class Monday, Tuesday, and Thursday with Grace Camp. Second group arrives at 10:50 and joins first group in gym.
11:00–11:35	Enter shared classroom. Circle time and story. Free play. Gary goes to Starr for lunches. Ruth washes dishes from morning snack and prepares for lunch.
11:35–11:45	Bathroom
1:45–12:15	Lunch in the gym. All staff except Gary eat with children. Special education gym class conducted in gym during lunch time.
12:15–12:45	Tooth brushing time (in the classroom and rest rooms). Children play with puzzles or look at books. Staff supervise tooth brushing. Ruth does dishes and cleans up lunch tables and kitchen.
12:45–1:00	Music in Gale Jolly's room, Monday, Tuesday, and Thursday.
1:00–1:30	Outside play or free play in room. Judy and Susan supervise indoor or outdoor play. Gary and Ruth take children from first group home.
1:30–2:20	Snack, art, and small group for second group. Susan prepares snack for second group. Snack and art located in classroom unless occupied.
2:30	Second group leaves for home. Gary and Ruth bring second group home. Judy and Susan clean room, prepare materials for next day, and complete daily paperwork.

FIGURE 4.1. Wood River Daily Schedule

cedures. The federal health team member left a copy of required topics with the Hoover CAC Head Start health component manager.

Following the report from the federal review team, the center- and home-based component managers reviewed the Performance Standards and developed a curriculum for center-based programs, consisting of both required and suggested topics. This list of education topics, combined with the health and safety topics, comprised the *Education Planning Guide*. The guide consisted of a month-by-month list of suggested themes and required activities, arranged by component area. Figure 4.2 shows the list for November. The double-starred activities were required to be completed during the assigned month and the single-starred activities were required to be completed during the program year. The date on which a required activity was completed was to be noted on the appropriate line on the Planning Guide. To assist teachers in planning the curriculum, the center- and home-based component managers and several Head Start teachers developed a resource guide divided by subject area that contained recipes, activity ideas, and theme-related material.

Each Thursday Judy and Susan planned the following week's lessons. During one week in early November when Judy was on vacation, Susan asked me if I would join her in planning the next week's activities.

Susan began, "Have you seen how we do this?" She took out the planning book and showed me how the activities were laid out day by day.

"The days are really a lot the same," she explained. "The art project changes. Other things, too. Anything starred is something that has to be done. Before we hand in the lesson plans, we have to highlight those things."

Susan also shared with me the Lesson Plans Yearly Program Requirements Sheet. Topics on this list included oral hygiene, shape recognition, visiting the dentist, and mealtime behavior. For each required item, Susan or Judy wrote down the date on which they presented the material to the children. As I looked through the lesson plan for the previous week, I noted that some items were starred, indicating that these were required topics, and that all hand washing and meal activities were recorded and starred.

Susan said, "Next week will be the letter *G*." She wrote this letter at the top of the week for the theme. Each week the program focused on one letter. This had begun in the second week of September with the letter *A*. The previous Head Start teacher, Luci Quist, had started the letter of the week, and Judy had continued the practice.

"Let's see," began Susan, "What could we do that starts with *G*? Germs and good manners?" Germs and good manners are both required topics to be covered each year.

I said, "Okay."

NOVEMBER
Suggested Themes: Community Helpers   Library
**Parent Conferences _____

EDUCATION
    Cognitive/Creative:
      *Color Recognition _____
      Body Shapes/Classification of Body Parts
    Communication:
      Recording Voices
    Cultural:
      Alike and Different
    Large Motor:
      Activities to Teach Body Parts (Head/Toes)
    Science:
      Space
    Small Motor:
      *Dressing Skills _____
      *Introduction to Pouring Skills _____

HEALTH
    Dental:
      **Awareness of the Mouth _____
    Nutrition:
      **Two Food Activities _____
      *Food Pyramid _____
    Physical Health:
      *Importance of Appropriate Clothing _____
      *Handicaps Awareness—Alike and Different _____
      *Germs (Coughing/Sneezing/Nose Blowing) _____
    Safety:
      **Fire Drill _____
      *Child Safety Protection Month
      (Body Rights, Child Protection, etc.) _____
    Self-Concept/Mental Health:
      *Who Am I—Alike and Different _____
      Body Tracing

PARENT INVOLVEMENT
    Child Protection Tips
    Homemade Games to Teach Colors
    **Dental Professional at Parent Meeting _____

SOCIAL SERVICE
    **Information about Available Christmas Projects _____
    (Put in Newsletter)

FIGURE 4.2. Center-Based Education Planning Guide. Double asterisk indicates activity to be completed during program month; single asterisk indicates activity to be completed during program year. Blank line is for completion dates.

Susan wrote *germs* and *good manners* in the lesson planning book, near the letter *G.*

She asked me to go over and look through the books for those on manners and germs. I went to look through the curriculum books located in the closet where the Head Start program had a number of early childhood curriculum books. I found some children's books and activity ideas related to manners, but none on germs.

"That's okay," responded Susan. "We could just talk about it during small-group time." She asked, "What stories could we do?"

I offered, "I have a gingerbread man pom-pom puppet, and I could do that story." I was thinking about the things I had at home that started with *G.*

"Okay, that would be good," said Susan, "We could do "Three Billy Goats Gruff," too. Maybe we could get a goat pattern; have them make a goat face."

I volunteered to bring some fake fur from home for the goat face. Susan wrote down the plan for the following week (see Figure 4.3), and we prepared to go home.

Judy and Susan planned the art projects and stories and finger-plays for group time around the weekly themes or an upcoming holiday. Before school, Judy and Susan would prepare for the art projects by cutting paper, tracing designs, and gathering all necessary materials, which they set up in the gym. Generally speaking, the art projects were adult directed: Judy presented a model, and staff helped children make the daily project. Occasionally Judy reprimanded a child who did not follow directions in making the project. She often used the same theme-related art projects year after year.

Maintaining the Facilities

Wood River Head Start, like other Hoover CAC Head Start programs, and all facilities licensed in the state as child care programs, is required to complete a daily site inspection form, which requires that bathrooms are cleaned daily, floors are mopped or vacuumed, files are locked, and emergency numbers are posted. Because Head Start was the only program licensed as a child care facility at the Early Learning Center, the family education and special education programs did not complete daily site inspections. At the start of the year, we assumed that Donna Blair, the janitor, was cleaning the bathrooms and classrooms. However, we quickly learned that this was not the case. When I checked with Gale Jolly, the special education teacher, about the bathrooms, she agreed that they were dirty and that this was a long-standing problem at the Early Learning Center.

One of my main duties was to supervise the boys' bathroom before lunch, and in late September a parent volunteer, Katie Lee, assisted me.

LESSON PLANS for Week of November 1-5th, 1993
G—Germs and Good Manners

Monday	Tuesday	Wednesday	Thursday
Greet children	Greet children	Greet children	Greet children
Check heads (lice)	Hand washing	Hand washing	Hand washing
Hand washing and bathroom	and bathroom	and bathroom	and bathroom
Snack	Snack	Snack	Snack
Art—goats	Art—gingerbread man	Fire drill	Art—paint on easel
Small group—songs and finger-plays	Small group—talk about germs	Small group—review fire drill	Small group—finger-plays with record
Second group arrives	*Second group arrives*	*Second group arrives*	*Second group arrives*
Exercise	Roll call	Roll call	Roll call
Roll call	Songs and finger-plays	Large group—make gingerbread cookies	Story—"Those Mean Nasty Dirty Downright Disgusting But Invisible Germs"
Story—"Three Billy Goats Gruff"	Story—"Gingerbread Man"	Story—"Clifford's Manners"	
Hand washing and bathroom	Hand washing and bathroom	Rug time—talk about good manners	Hand washing and bathroom
Lunch	Lunch	Hand washing and bathroom	Lunch
Tooth brushing	Tooth brushing	Lunch	Tooth brushing
		Tooth brushing	
Afternoon	*Afternoon*	*Afternoon*	*Afternoon*
Free choice	Books and puzzles	Outside play time	Music
Music	Music	First group home	Outside walk
Large group—"Ring Around the Rosey"	First group home	Bathroom and hand washing	First group home
First group home	Bathroom and hand washing	Snack	Bathroom and hand washing
Check heads (lice)	Snack	Fire drill	Snack
Bathroom and hand washing	Art	Small group—review fire drill	Art
Snack	Small group	*Second group home*	Records and finger-plays
Art	*Second group home*		*Second group home*
Small group			
Second group home			

FIGURE 4.3. Weekly Lesson Plan

When we came out of the rest room, she said, "That room smelled something awful." Judy replied that it did not bother her. Two weeks later, in preparation for the building-wide open house, Judy and Susan cleaned both the girls' and boys' bathrooms. Following the open house, Judy asked Donna for some air fresheners for the rest rooms. Judy remarked, "The bathrooms don't seem good; I cleaned them yesterday."

Donna responded, "I wondered who did that."

Susan emptied the trash from the classroom, rest rooms, and kitchen on a daily basis. On days when Head Start didn't operate and the family education program did, Susan would return to find the classroom trash cans overflowing. In October Judy commented on a "rotten smell" in the room. After checking the trash cans, she checked the adjoining room, which was used as a diaper-changing area by parents enrolled in family education classes. The bathroom trash contained several soiled diapers, which Judy then emptied in the dumpster outside. She later said, "Donna is supposed to be emptying the trash."

In some instances Judy or Susan would leave a note for Donna to fill the paper-towel containers or wash the area of the gym floor near the lunch tables. Judy said, "I feel like such a nag, leaving notes like this." When Judy or Susan left notes, Donna usually filled the paper-towel containers or washed the floors. At other times, Judy, Susan, Ruth, and I did the tasks ourselves. One morning, after Judy had left a note asking Donna to wash the gym and kitchen floors, I asked Susan if the floors were clean.

Susan responded, "I came in this morning, and it was dirty. Donna came in and said she would do that. I told her that since we mess it up, I would clean it."

Susan compared building maintenance at the Early Learning Center with that at St. John's. In early October she and I carried art supplies from the gym to the classroom. Susan looked at the carpeting in the classroom and said, "I don't know if Donna vacuums it every day or not. It doesn't look like she does it."

I responded, "No."

Susan added, "It is like at St. John's. They didn't take good care of the rooms and clean them up."

Later that month Susan showed me the site inspection form that she had completed in the morning, which included checking that the bathrooms, kitchen, and eating areas are cleaned daily. When Susan showed me this form, I asked her, "What would happen if you didn't check that? We really don't think that those bathrooms are cleaned every day."

Susan said, "I am not sure, and we don't know if Donna is doing them or not. Compared to St. John's, this isn't bad. There the janitor did them in the morning, and then the older kids would come down and clog up the toilets. It was a real mess."

Building maintenance continued to be a problem, so Judy asked Hoover CAC to extend Susan's hours so that she could complete the daily cleaning. In April, at Judy's request, Hoover CAC extended Susan's hours so that she was paid to clean the classroom, bathrooms, and gym floor.

EXAMINING POLICY IMPLICATIONS

Power Distribution

The results of the federal review prompted Ann to move the Wood River program to a new location. Judy requested that Ann apply for a year variance so that the program could stay at St. John's until a mobile unit was constructed. However, Ann overruled Judy's request and began negotiations with the school district to rent space in the Early Learning Center.

There are several possibilities why Ann overruled Judy's request. Even if Ann had applied for the variance, federal supervisors may have denied the request. Another possibility is that Judy's positionality, or relationship to Ann, her boss, made it difficult for her to press her request for the variance. Judy, in speaking with Ann about the variance, may have made her request and then decided that she did not have the authority to press further. In talking with me and other Wood River staff about the variance, Judy may have been more vocal about her discomfort with Ann's decision because she was more comfortable discussing the problem with familiar staff than with her boss (Ceglowski & Seem, 1994). Judy both questioned and accepted Ann's authority to overrule her variance request.

Another explanation for Ann's overruling Judy's request is that policies such as site-based management, designed to insure local input, emanate from central authority structures that are "prone to delegate tasks, but they are not inclined to redistribute power" (Malen, 1994, p. 250). Judy, vested with the responsibility for overseeing the daily operations of the program, best knew the impact on the program of the negotiations. It seems logical that Judy, positioned as the site-based manager at Wood River, should have the power and authority to request that Hoover CAC apply for the variance. Site-based management increased Judy's responsibilities but did not delegate additional power or authority to the local site.

Significance of Differences Between Programs

Until the negotiations with the school district, Judy had little contact with
the Early Learning Center programs. Wood River, like many other Head
Start programs, operated separately from other early childhood programs
and was not well integrated with any of the Early Learning Center programs.
This long-established pattern, begun during the founding days of Head Start,
reflected the 1960s federal government distrust of state governments to provide adequate services to children and families. Recognizing that it was bene-
ficial for Head Start to work closely with other early childhood programs,
authors of the 1994 Head Start Reauthorization Bill included a directive for
grantees to collaborate with other community early childhood programs.

Wood River began the year on unequal footing with other Early Learning Center programs and operated under a different administrative system
and set of policies. Though the kindergarten, special education, and family
education programs each serves specific populations and has entry requirements, they are all administered by the Starr–Wood River School District.
Staff in these programs are required to have state teaching licenses, are evaluated by Starr–Wood River administrators, and are paid by the school district.
The three programs followed the same calendar, and two of the programs,
special education and kindergarten, operated their two daily sessions during
the same time periods. Wood River Head Start teaching staff, like other Hoover CAC Head Start staff, were CDA certified, supervised by agency administrators, and paid on the Hoover CAC salary schedule. Hoover CAC determined the yearly calendar, personnel policies, and program requirements.

The Early Learning Center and Head Start staffs noted the disparities
between the organizational and operating structure of the programs. The
dirty bathroom situation, described in this chapter, is a case in point. State
child care licensing regulations, which applied only to Head Start and not to
the special education or family education programs, required that staff clean
the bathrooms and eating areas daily. The special education staff agreed with
Head Start that the janitor should clean the bathrooms, but they did not
press the issue with the school district.

The special education teacher, Gale, asked me why Head Start teachers
did not have teaching licenses. In public school programs, it is assumed that
teachers have licenses, and it was difficult for Gale to understand why Head
Start teachers are not required to do the same. After I explained to her how
Head Start is structured, she continued to ask questions about the difference
in teacher qualifications. Perhaps she perceived this difference in terms of
the quality of teaching and caliber of the Head Start teaching staff. Despite Gale's feelings about the Head Start staff, she made the most concerted

effort to collaborate with the program staff. These efforts are discussed in Chapter 8.

Compliance with Prescriptive Policies

In planning the Head Start program around that of the other programs, Judy and Susan complied with Hoover CAC curriculum requirements. Several factors influenced lesson planning at Wood River—the curriculum topics mandated by Hoover CAC, the lack of permanent classroom space, and Judy's philosophy of working with children.

In thinking about lesson planning with Susan, I began to understand how influential the annual and monthly required topics were in determining the daily curriculum. In interviews for a previous study (Ceglowski, 1994), Hoover CAC teachers had told me that the prescribed curriculum negatively affected their sense of professionalism. They wondered why they were required to obtain training when they were then told what to teach. I asked myself a question that first occurred to me during my second day at Wood River: Do mandates become the curriculum? In the case of lesson planning, it seemed that Susan and Judy used the required topics as the basis for determining the focus for their written curriculum. Prescriptive policies, such as that of the monthly topics, require that staff follow certain prescriptions to meet stated goals and objectives. Prescriptive policies are based on the premise that centralized decision making and monitoring are essential in standardizing certain characteristics of local programs, including services provided and staff qualifications (Weiler, 1990).

Judy and Susan complied with Hoover CAC curriculum requirements when they developed and submitted weekly lesson plans. They often completed the lesson plans as a procedural matter rather than as a reflection of the daily occurrences at the program. In other words, when Judy and Susan completed and sent in the weekly lesson plans, they were signaling to the Hoover CAC administrators that the program was doing what Head Start programs do. The Wood River staff, when completing the required paperwork, was exhibiting procedural engagement (see Nystrand & Gamoran, 1991). The phrase "procedural engagement" refers to how local staff orient themselves toward the requirements to follow the rules and regulations established by program administrators with the aim of maintaining uniformity in policy compliance. Judy's weekly lesson plans were procedural displays (DeStefano & Pepinksi, 1981) indicating to Hoover CAC that she had followed the required curriculum.

Another procedural display was the classroom checklist that Susan completed each day by checking off, among other things, that the bathrooms and kitchen were cleaned daily. When I questioned Susan about this, noting that the bathrooms and kitchen were not clean, she compared the Early Learning Center bathrooms to those at St. John's, where the elementary school children messed them up as soon as the janitor cleaned them. When Hoover CAC administrators inspected the program, they did not note that the bathrooms were in need of cleaning. It was only after Judy requested that Susan's hours be extended and Hoover CAC approved the request in the spring of 1994 that the bathrooms were cleaned on a regular basis. As Susan explained to me, "We are using the bathrooms; we should clean them."

Procedural displays indicate to Hoover CAC administrators that Wood River staff are doing things the "Head Start way." Tyack & Tobin (1994) define this consistency in school practices as the "grammar" of schooling. The Wood River staff, familiarized with the grammar of Hoover CAC Head Start, established patterns of completing paperwork and doing things the Head Start way, not for its local utility but because administrators monitor their activities by reviewing paperwork and conducting on-site reviews.

Official Curriculum and Program Implementation

In addition to their compliance with prescriptive policies, staff's philosophies influenced how they developed and implemented the daily program. On several occasions, Judy complained about the required themes and said that what was really important at Head Start was for children to learn to socialize. At Wood River, socialization times included meals, free play time, and outside play time. During these times, adults enforced minimal rules, and children were free to interact with one other. The other portions of the day were more teacher directed: art, music, and group time. During these times children were reminded that teachers were in charge, and those children who did not attend to the activities were first redirected and then temporarily removed from the group.

In thinking about the planned curriculum at Wood River and comparing it to developmentally appropriate practice, described in the prevailing "best practices" literature published by the National Association for the Education of Young Children (Bredekamp & Copple, 1997), I surmised that the curriculum was more staff selected and directed than was often recommended. For instance, early childhood best practices stress the importance of learning centers that allow children to make choices among several activities. Teachers are advised to plan at least 45 minutes for this free play time and during this period move from center to center, facilitating children's play and conversing with children. I had incorporated this approach in my teaching and was at first disappointed that Wood River staff did not use learning centers. Free play at Wood River was a different matter. During this time, which did not occur every day and varied in length, children were "free" to play in the housekeeping area, with art supplies, puzzles, blocks, toys, trucks, and games. The materials did not vary significantly during the year, and staff did not set up special activities on a daily basis. During free play, adults often caught up on paperwork, made return phone calls, chatted, and sometimes sat and played with the children. This pattern seemed to work well at Wood River and became the free play routine. I realized how entrenched this pattern was when, on one occasion, while Judy was on vacation and Susan was completing the end-of-the-month paperwork, I set up a number of winter holiday learning centers that included easel painting, tracing, a matching game, and an art station. My intent was that the children could use these materials during free play time.

Luke, a lively 4-year-old, moved from activity to activity, painting a picture at the easel and making a card for his mother. At the end of the hour-long session, when I told the children that it was time to clean up, he came and asked me, "When are we going to play?" Luke's comment alerted me that I had violated the notion of free play in the classroom. Play, although valued at Wood River, had a different tone to it than that to which I was accustomed.

Yet the official curriculum, which included the daily lesson plans and written records, provides a limited view of what occurred at Wood River. Washing hands, eating, and changing rooms took up the lion's share of the 2.5-hour session. Wood River, like other center-based Head Start programs, provides children with two thirds of their daily caloric intake. As required by federal and agency policy, staff provided 1.5 hours between snack and lunch. When the first group of children arrived at 10, they immediately washed their hands for snack and began eating. At 11:30, children in both groups washed for lunch, which was served at 11:45. As required by Head Start Performance Standards, children brushed their teeth after lunch. At 1:30, children in the second group washed their hands and ate snack.

Moving children to and from the bathroom, gym, and classroom for meals and tooth brushing took considerable time. Judy, Susan, and I took turns supervising the boys' and girls' rest rooms and lining the children up outside the bathrooms to walk to the gym for meals. In my previous teaching positions, lining up was not a skill that was stressed, because either many of the classrooms contained bathrooms or the staff did not believe that lining up was an essential preschool skill. At Wood River Judy decided that it was important to teach lining up and walking in a line, and by Christmas time I found myself telling children to line up and reminding them to use their "walking feet" when in the hall. Before Christmas in 1993 I was substituting for Judy and kept track of eight times when Susan and I lined the children up to move from room to room. My observation was substantiated by a parent evaluator from a different Hoover CAC Head Start program when she commented after visiting Wood River, "All they do is line up and move from one place to another!"

Judy and Susan worked against numerous obstacles to develop the Head Start program at the Early Learning Center. Head Start did not enjoy the same access to rooms and resources as the other Early Learning Center programs. Differences between Head Start policies and those of the public school led to conflicts throughout the school year. As in the past, Wood River staff complied with required curriculum topics and documentation of daily activities.

Before the beginning of the program year, as required by Hoover CAC policy, Judy visited all incoming children and their families at home. The staff knew some of the families because older siblings had attended the program. Other children had attended during the previous year and were returning for their 2nd year of Head Start. As the children entered the program, the Wood River staff got to know the Head Start families and children. In the following chapter I describe the Wood River children and families.

5

Research as Relationship: The Wood River Head Start Families

THE FARM BOYS

Throughout the summer of 1993, Martha Calle, the Wood River County supervisor, and I met at the Wood River Kwik Trip for a daily walk. Martha lived 11 miles away in Carleton. On the way to Carleton she faced two major road construction projects going on that summer, so it took her 20 minutes to drive to Wood River. I lived only six miles away, but my children were at home, and this was the best meeting place that we could find.

That summer was coolish with a few spots of humid weather, but we met, drizzle or shine, and walked through mist or sweat. Martha talked about her job, telling stories of the teachers she supervised and the paperwork she had to fill out. Since I was, at that time, studying for my doctoral comprehensive examinations, I listened to Martha, glad for a change of pace from book learning.

We always followed the same route, crossing the street from the Kwik Trip and heading over the Wood River bridge, following the county road as it wound first along the river, and then into the lower farm country. After the bridge was the worm farm with the old black lab that barked when we passed by. Martha laughed at him and yelled, "We won't eat your worms!" Farther up on the right side was a ginger tiger cat and her latest ginger litter, who followed us up the road. "Go back!" I would say, afraid that the kittens would be hit by a car. A skinny black dog, coated with prickers, trotted down from a hilly driveway and followed along with the cats. Then we usually walked on, the Wood River moving fast and dirty below and the hills rising on our left. The snakes lay thick on the side of the road, waiting for the frogs that crossed from the side waters to the river's edge. I'm snake skittish so Martha would always walk by the side of the road. The flowers started with daisy whites in June and ended in September with the pungent odor of wild aster and goldenrod.

As we walked that summer I usually looked for the farm round the bend, the last one before the horse farm. For at that farm the boys would be out in the yard, four tow-headed young ones ranging in age from maybe 4 to 10. Barefoot and bare chested, they swung from ropes hung from the trees or pushed each other around on an old wagon with a wooden box placed inside. On the days we walked they were usually there, outside, morning or evening. On occasion we waved to them, and sometimes they stopped and looked at us before they went back to their play.

In the nearby barn or in the field across the way, their father worked the land or milked the cows. Blonde, like his sons, he was always nearby but busy. He spread manure, led the cows to the pasture, and plowed the field.

The barn stood a short muddy distance from the farmhouse, which had the look of rural poverty, the wood gray and in need of paint and repair. In the evening hours the barn echoed with the *moos* of cows at the stanchions. Otherwise, it stood empty, doors wide open, smelling of manure.

So the farm boys became a marker of this walk, a place to reach, just like the querulous lab at the worm farm and the tiger cats. As September began, the boys weren't always outside, since school had begun. Martha's and my walks became less regular. She was back to work full-time with the program year starting up, and I began my volunteer work at the Wood River Head Start program, determined to write my way through a dissertation. Daily I drove past the road on which Martha and I had walked most days that summer.

One day I spoke to the Wood River Head Start bus driver, Gary, asking where he picked up the Head Start children, and he told me about one child who came from the road near the Wood River. "Farm family?" I asked. "Yeah, not too far up the road from the Kwik Trip," he told me. I looked out in the group and found a tow-headed boy, Steven. A quiet and well-behaved child, he and I often sat near each other during breakfast. I then placed him as one of the boys we saw at the farm. In my mind's eye, I saw him outside, barefoot and bare chested, with his brothers during the summer. One day I said to him, "Did you ever see me walk past your house?" He shook his head.

"I saw you and your brothers outside playing with ropes and things." Steven looked at me.

Later that week Steven brought a broken toy pistol to school, stuck in the waist of his pants. Another child told him to put it in his bag, because "you can't have guns here." Steven had the gun out in the boy's rest room, showing it to the other 4-year-olds.

Judy told me that Steven lived with his grandma and grandpa because his dad had gone back to school full-time in Northwind. Sometime before, his mother had left her husband and sons. Steven didn't talk about his mom or dad, but at breakfast he tells me about his grandma. "She works in the apple orchard." Two days later Wood River Head Start went to the orchard, and I asked, "Who is Steven's grandma?" Someone pointed out a heavyset woman in an old dress and baggy red sweater who was sorting apples. She doesn't speak to the children as they passed, but she laughed shyly when I took her picture. Steven told me that sometimes "Grandma brings us apples home from here."

During school, Steven played with the other boys, sitting next to Luke at meals. They giggled and peered under the table. "Boys, sit up and eat," called Judy, sitting a few seats away. After lunch, when Judy asked what a tornado could do, Steven said, "Blow down the barn."

"That's right; did you hear what he said?" responded Judy.

During singing, Steven sat quietly, and when we went next door to join the other class for music, he hid his head in his lap, and stayed that way for 20 minutes. "Don't worry about that," said Judy. "He was like that when he came here. He'll get over it in time." We all waited for that time to come.

Later in October Martha and I walked our old summer route again. The flowers were fading; only the asters looked bright on the hills, and the oaks had turned to russet. We went past the worm farm. Martha called to the dog, "Eat 'em yourself." The kittens had grown and found farms far from here. The skinny black dog followed us again as we rounded the bend toward the farm boys' place. No bare-chested and barefoot ones around. It was chilly and looked like rain. In the window, a boy looked toward us. He was dressed in a sweater and jeans, school clothes. I lifted my arm to wave to him, and he waved back. The next day I told Steven that I had waved at his brother. "I know," he replied, "I saw you walking there, too."

As in the case of Steven, this research project drew me into the lives of people who were geographically close but unknown to me. I "discovered the once invisible [people] who lived throughout" (Weinstein-Shr, 1992, p. 166), in my case children and families living in poverty. These families I found were living down the block from me or, like Steven, on a farm that I passed every day. Though I had worked with Hoover CAC staff for over a decade, I had had little contact with the children and families whom they served. I realized soon after arriving at Wood River that it was my relationships with the staff, children, and parents that were the key to understanding how the program operated. This relational understanding, which I call "research as relationship," is manifest in personal biographies, daily conversations, and the mundane and extraordinary activities at the center. My research agenda, to study how policies are interpreted, was nested in my relationships with the Wood River children, families, staff, and Hoover CAC administrators.

When I joined the Wood River community and learned to volunteer, I entered what Lave and Wenger (1991) call a community of practice. Individuals belong to various communities of practice, which sanction certain ways of acting and talking. I joined the Wood River staff with multiple community memberships, including teacher, parent, researcher, and Hoover CAC consultant. Entry into my role as a volunteer began by learning from established members of the Wood River staff the knowledge and skills necessary for full participation in the daily events at the program. As newcomers engage in activities and conversations with community members, they negotiate and renegotiate how to participate in the daily events and what participation means in the context of that specific community (Lave & Wenger, 1991).

How I negotiated and renegotiated my membership with the Wood River staff, or my positionality in that context, was an ongoing process in this research project. How the Wood River staff, children, parents, and Hoover CAC administrative staff described my membership in the Wood River community changed and shifted over time. These shiftings occurred in the context of activities and conversations with the Wood River staff and Hoover CAC administrators.

My membership in the research community was, at times, in conflict with my membership in the Wood River staff community. For instance, when Judy asked me what I thought about a policy, I replied that first I wanted to know what she thought about it. She turned to me and said, "That is what you always say, this time I want to know what you think!" In this interaction, I recognized that my positioning as a researcher, someone who avoids giving opinions, was in tension with my positioning as a volunteer staff member.

Judy knew that I had worked with other Hoover CAC Head Start programs, consulting with staff regarding problem situations. She told me at the start of the year that she did not think that the Hoover CAC administrators would visit as much that year; they would expect me to keep an eye on things. Several administrators did ask me how things were going at Wood River, and I would respond with nonjudgmental statements, commenting on the activities we were doing. Judy also described me as an "extra pair of hands." She said that it had become easier for Susan and her, now that I was around. On the day that Judy added my name and phone number to the posted staff list, I felt like an accepted member of the Wood River community. Yet a Hoover CAC administrator viewed my position differently, stating that "it must be hard for Judy, knowing that you are there every day" as a researcher. How others positioned me as a spy, evaluator, "extra pair of hands," or intimidator was influenced by my previous history with Hoover CAC, and how familiar individuals were with my daily work at the program.

THE HEAD START CHILDREN AND THEIR FAMILIES

The Wood River Head Start families, like all families, varied in their composition, strengths, support networks, and problems. Some families provided their children with warm and nurturing homes, whereas others struggled with chemical dependence, unemployment, and incarceration. This diversity was manifest in a comment made during my 2nd year at the program by 3-year-old Jacob. Jacob was then living with his grandparents because his mother was in a treatment program and his father was in prison. Every day Jacob watched as Tom's mother, and sometimes his dad, brought him out to the bus (sometimes carrying him) and hugged him before he got aboard. One day Jacob told Ruth, the bus rider, "Wish I could go ta Tim's. His mom could do tha' for me."

Though Steven had warm and nurturing grandparents, he would talk about how much he missed his mother and father. He occasionally told Judy and me that he "missed his mom every day." In January, he told us that he and his brothers would be visiting his mother and how much he was looking forward to the visit. Other children who lived with one parent talked about how much they missed their noncustodial parent. Sarah, whose parents had recently divorced, cried often despite staff's efforts to console her.

Though Head Start children and their families were diverse, one common thread ran throughout this population—poverty. Most Head Start families, and all of the Wood River Head Start families, lived below federal poverty guidelines. In 1996, an income-eligible family of four could earn no more than $15,600. As in the case of Ben's family, which consisted of his mother and brother, many families had monthly incomes substantially below this level. At the start of the year, Ben wore white shoes with holes on the side. In October, he came to school in purple boots. Despite Susan's constant reminders to bring shoes, Ben arrived in his purple boots. One day I asked about Ben's family and was told that his mother received $800 per month in welfare payments, food stamps, and health benefits to support herself and her two sons.

Of the 17 children enrolled in 1993–94, 6 came from families with fathers and mothers both present. In several of these families, both parents were working, sometimes full-time. For those children living in single-parent homes, most of the custodial parents either worked or, like Ben's mother, were full-time students. Philip's mother, who supported herself and her three sons, worked three jobs to "make ends meet."

Getting Acquainted

Families interested in registering for Head Start applied through the Hoover CAC Head Start office. The office staff determined which families qualified for the program and then sent Judy a class list. In a few instances the Hoover CAC office staff, unfamiliar with the bus route boundaries, enrolled families living outside the transportation area, which included three towns and some of the surrounding area, but did not enroll families from more remote regions. People living farther out of town had the choice of transporting their children to and from the closest bus stop or withdrawing their application for the program. Judy suggested that if Hoover CAC checked with her before they enrolled the families, she could verify whether the family lived in a bus service area. In some instances, parents chose not to enroll their children in Head Start because they could not arrange their work schedules around that of the Head Start schedule.

Once families were enrolled in the Wood River program, the staff learned about them and their children through informal and planned means. In some cases, older brothers and sisters had attended Head Start, and staff had already developed a relationship with the family. Sometimes Judy, an established resident of the area, knew of a family. Most often, she met a new family during a home visit scheduled prior to the start of the fall session. During this time, she introduced herself to the parents and children, reviewed a parent handbook, and helped parents complete required paperwork. Amanda Red, a Hoover CAC family advocate who provided social services to Head Start families in three counties, conducted a home visit to each family prior to the child's entry in the Head Start program. Amanda completed a family needs assessment that listed both the family's strengths and its goals for the upcoming year and outlined the services she could provide to the family.

Parents then attended an orientation session before the fall program began. During this session, staff introduced themselves, reviewed bus rules and regulations, described the daily program, and answered questions. The first day of the fall session consisted of an open house that parents and children attended together. During this time, children played in the classroom and staff chatted with parents.

Keeping in Touch with Parents

Some parents visited during the first week to check on their children. Carla Lueck called and visited because her 3-year-old son, Kevin, cried when Gary and Ruth picked him up for school. She asked Judy on the 1st day, "Is he still crying?" Judy assured her that by the time he got to school he had calmed down. On the 2nd day of school when she visited, Carla asked, "Is he acting like a little monster?" Judy laughed and visited with Carla while the children played on the playground. Another parent, Brenda Younger, stopped by with her toddler daughter to check in on her older daughter, Bonnie. Judy first explained the policy, stating that children under 3 were not allowed in the classroom, but then added that "it would be fine" for her to stop in for a visit. Brenda volunteered to help in the program and frequently assisted in the classroom, on field trips, and when staff were absent. Other parents volunteered as well, though the number of volunteer hours had drastically decreased because most parents were working during the day.

Other parents stopped by—some on a regular basis and others unannounced. On the 2 days per week that Gina Down picked her son Ben up early, Judy or another staff member would talk to her for a few minutes as Ben got ready to leave. Lisa King would stop in during the day occasionally and join us for lunch, outdoor play time, or circle time.

Ruth and Gary had daily contact with most of the parents and carried information to and from the children's homes to school. Before I substituted for Ruth and learned more about both her job and Gary's, I had considered bus drivers and riders as related but not central figures in the Head Start program. However, as I got to know more about what they did, I changed my thinking about their roles in the program.

It was Ruth and Gary who talked with the parents as they brought their children to the bus and picked them up in the afternoon. For many of the children in this rural area, their daily bus ride to and from school was nearly as long as their time in the classroom. Ruth had established a policy of sitting and talking with each child from when they got on the bus until the next stop.

Parents called Gary or Ruth before school to tell them if their children were sick and would not be attending the program that day. During the school day parents called frequently, and working parents called Judy at home in the evening. Staff called parents if they had questions or concerns about the children, and parents often called the staff to report a sick child or changes in the family or to ask for information about the program schedule.

Formal Communications with Parents

Formal communications with parents included the two required home visits planned for the beginning and end of the program year, fall and spring parent-teacher conferences, and written correspondence. During the initial home visit, Judy met the family and described the program, and at the end-of-the-year visit, she consulted with the family about their children's progress and the family's plans for the upcoming year. At the parent-teacher conferences in the fall and spring, Judy gave a report of children's progress at Wood River and shared the results of a basic skill inventory that assessed children's understanding of color, shapes, numbers, letters, and sequencing. Parents shared information about the family and concerns about their children.

Staff wrote notes and newsletters and photocopied and distributed communications from Hoover CAC. Judy or Susan sent notes to parents to remind them to send extra clothing or supplies, to return forms, or to inform them that a child was injured or had been exposed to a communicable disease. Staff wrote monthly newsletters describing current projects and upcoming events. Material from Hoover CAC included information on local resources, changes in the Head Start program, and parenting information.

PARENT PARTICIPATION AT WOOD RIVER

Federal policy stipulates that all local Head Start programs establish a Head Start Parent Committee comprising parents whose children are currently enrolled in the program. The committee members' responsibilities are to work with the teaching staff in planning and operating the program, to participate in ongoing parenting activities, and to assist the program in screening and selecting new staff members. The committee also elected one parent to serve on the Hoover CAC Head Start Policy Council. The policy council met monthly to review and approve budgets, policies, and staff appointments.

On September 21, 1993, thirteen parents attended a Head Start committee meeting, referred to by staff as a parent meeting. During this meeting, Susan and Ruth cared for the Head Start children and their siblings in the classroom. Amanda Red, the family advocate, moderated the meeting. Amanda handed out a sheet that described the Head Start committee structure and officer positions of chair, vice chair, secretary, and treasurer, and that of representative to the Hoover CAC Head Start Policy Council.

Judy then introduced Kathryn Shay as someone "who serves on the Hoover CAC Head Start Policy Council and before that served on the Wood River Parent Committee." Kathryn described the policy council as "a place where it's fun to feel the power under your belt." Kathryn explained that the policy council members get to make decisions about the program. They voted on and approved budgets and assisted in preparing for the federal review. "At first," she said, "you don't think that you can do the job." She told the parents that they got reimbursed for mileage and child care and that they didn't have to report this income on their Aid for Families with Dependent Children form. She ended by saying that she hoped that one of the parents would volunteer to serve on the policy council.

Amanda ended the presentation on the committee positions and that of policy council representative by saying, "These offices don't take a lot of time, and they can be a lot of fun. Next time we are going to elect officers." At the next meeting in October, eight parents and one grandparent attended. Parents volunteered for the Wood River Center Parent Committee officer positions and to be the Hoover CAC Head Start Policy Council representative.

Parent Education

Head Start policy mandates that each program develop a parent education plan based upon the needs of the parents. At the first parent meeting in

September, Amanda Red distributed an interest survey to the parents. The parents checked off those topics they wanted to discuss during the monthly meetings. Judy then told the parents that she had arranged for the next 2 months' guest speakers. A nurse would speak on first aid at the October meeting, and a dentist would speak on dental health at the November meeting. Amanda explained, "These are the required-topic meetings. But after these meetings, you can decide what you want to talk about." As it turned out in Wood River, parents chose only one of the topics for the 1993–94 parent education topics. In December Kathryn asked Judy if she could speak on sexual abuse, and Hoover CAC instituted a parenting series that staff planned for January, February, and March. The last scheduled parent meeting in April included a presentation on discipline, a topic that many parents requested.

The guest speakers for the parent meetings were arranged by either Judy or Amanda. Amanda said that she would meet with the newly elected chair, Lisa King, before each meeting to plan the agenda for the meeting. Hoover CAC policy stipulates that it is the responsibility of the family advocate to train and mentor local Head Start Parent Committee officers.

A. The Family Advocates are responsible for providing training and support to the parent officers.
B. Training and information will be provided on conducting meetings according to Roberts [sic] Rules of Order. The Family Advocate may facilitate group training for this purpose.
C. The Family Advocates are responsible for personally meeting with the Parent Chairpersons monthly, two weeks prior to the upcoming meeting to establish a written agenda.
D. The Family Advocates will assist the Parent Chairperson in locating and arranging for speaker and/or training at each parent meeting.
E. Some type of parent education/training shall be provided at each parent meeting. References should be made to the Parent Meeting Topic and Interest Form and the components of the Head Start program (Hoover CAC, 1993a, p. 61).

Later in the year Amanda reported that she and Lisa had difficulty getting together for a planning time and hadn't been able to do so during the year.

Parent Meetings

Judy sent out reminder notes before each parent meeting, along with copies of the minutes of the last meeting. Most meetings were scheduled for Tuesdays from 7:00 to 8:30 P.M. Seven parents regularly attended the monthly meetings: Lisa King, the committee chair; Jane Short, the vice chair; Katie

Lee, the secretary and policy council representative; and four others. Amanda Red began each meeting with some introductory comments, followed by Katie Lee first reading and then the parents voting to approve the minutes of the previous meeting. Judy talked about upcoming events such as field trips, parent conferences, and no-school days.

Before each monthly parent education presentation, Amanda asked parents if they had any questions or concerns. At the October parent meeting, Jane Short, a vocal mother in the group, asked Amanda if the parent group was going to have a fund-raiser this year. Amanda responded, "I'm not sure that we are going to have them this year. If we do, there is a good chance that we have to have an audit. I am not sure about this, but there is a possibility that the parent group will get an activity allotment for the year."

Jane asked, "Does this mean that we can't do a fund-raiser?"

Amanda answered, "Well, if the group decided that it wanted to do a fund-raiser, then we would have to work it out. I'm not saying that you couldn't do a fund-raiser."

At the February parent meeting Jane asked about fund-raisers again and Amanda told her, "The office isn't encouraging them this year." The Wood River parent group did not sponsor a fund-raiser during the 1993–94 year. In reviewing Hoover CAC policies, I learned that Wood River parents could choose to have a fund-raiser as long as the event was approved by the Hoover CAC Head Start Policy Council. The policy on fund-raisers stated that the local parent group was entitled to 20% of any proceeds, with the remaining 80% going to the policy council.

That year, more parents attended the March meeting than any other. Judy attributed this higher attendance to the free pizza-and-soda dinner that the program provided to the families. Judy paid for the pizza with funds allocated by Hoover CAC for a special parent education series that included the topics at February and March meetings.

EXAMINING POLICY IMPLICATIONS

Interactions with Parents

Judy prided herself on the rapport she developed with parents. She had a matter-of-fact way of talking that let people know what she was thinking. After listening to Judy talk to parents on the phone for 2 years, I can still hear, "Hello, Lisa, this is Judy. How are you doing? Oh." (And she would listen). "Say, the reason I'm calling is about that form we sent home. Did you get it?"

Judy's way of communicating with parents and dealing with children was different from my own. In Brian, a 4-year-old enrolled in the program, I saw a younger version of my own son, James, and at the same time recognized the poverty that separated my son from him. Throughout the year I struggled with the disparity between my own situation and that of the children. In dubbing me "soft heart," Judy pinpointed a difference in how we perceived the children and their families. I noted that Wood River provided a center-based program for children such as Brian and family support services for parents such as Katie Lee, but it did not alter the life situation for this family. Judy, a former Head Start parent who had started out as a volunteer at Wood River, had a more pragmatic approach to the children and their parents. She provided a consistent and safe environment for the children and expected their parents to support them. Combined with her matter-of-fact talking style was Judy's respect for parents' rights to make decisions affecting their children. Though the staff might not agree with the parents' decisions, Judy always reminded us that it was the parent who was responsible for the child's well-being.

Limited Power of Parents

Parent involvement is a cornerstone of the initial plan for Head Start. Preceding the publication of the performance standards by 14 years, *The Head Start Policy Manual: The Parents,* referred to by Head Start personnel as 70.2, delineates four types of parent involvement in local programs:

1. Participation in the process of making decisions about the nature and operation of the program
2. Participation in the classroom as paid employees, volunteers, or observers
3. Activities for the parents which they have helped to develop
4. Working with their children in cooperation with the staff of the center (U.S. DHHS, 1970, p. 2)

In 1993–94, the authority of the Wood River Committee to make decisions affecting the parent group's functions appeared limited. In the only instance when a program parent, Jane, made a suggestion for a parent activity, Amanda first told her that they "could work out" the fund-raiser suggestion, and then, when Jane raised the question again 4 months later, Amanda said that the "office wasn't encouraging them" for that year. When I asked Martha Calle about it, she told me that the parent committee would need to obtain policy council approval, but it was possible to plan a fund-raiser.

There are several reasons why the parents had limited power. First, the officers were new to their roles and received limited training and no mentoring for their positions. Second, Katie Lee, the policy council representative, did not attend the policy council meetings regularly and did not review policy council business at the parent meetings. If she had been able to attend policy council meetings, she might have become active in Head Start decision making. Third, Amanda, who served Head Start families in three counties, did not provide training and mentoring to officers or the Wood River Parent Committee. She was unable to meet with the committee officers to plan the agenda and arrange guest speakers. Consequently, Judy and Amanda made the arrangements for all the guest speakers, and Amanda facilitated most of the parent meetings. And fourth, the required parent education topics and mandated special parent education series limited parent choice for the monthly topics.

The report from the Advisory Committee on Head Start Quality and Expansion (U.S. DHHS, 1993a) recommended that local programs evaluate their parent involvement component and "make renewed efforts to include parents as decisionmakers, volunteers, and the primary educators of their children" (p. 43). The committee further recommends that local programs provide training for center committee and policy council members to "participate effectively and help make informed decisions about all program issues" (p. 44). Two related points from the advisory committee's recommendations are pertinent to Wood River—parents as decision makers and training for local committees.

As I sat at the parent meetings during 1993–94, it was difficult to determine whether parents' lack of training impeded their ability to make local decisions or whether the decision making available to parents was so limited that regardless of how much training they received, they would not be vested with the authority to make significant decisions affecting the program. Perhaps the best way for programs to approach this dilemma is to work on both possibilities simultaneously—providing ongoing training and mentoring to committee members and reviewing the opportunities for parent groups to make meaningful decisions about the program. Although Amanda had a responsibility for providing the training, this did not occur. Perhaps Hoover CAC could enlist the expertise of Kathryn Shay, a former Head Start parent and current member of the policy council, to assist in training and mentoring of committee officers and the policy council representative.

In tandem with the training and mentoring comes an examination of the decision-making power of the local center committees. As stated in 70.2, the committee's responsibilities include assisting the center staff in "the development and operation of every component including curriculum," working with the staff to "carry out the daily activities program," helping to develop and implement programs for parents, and assisting in "recruiting and screening" of staff (U.S. DHHS, 1970, pp. 5–6). Yet when Jane asked Amanda about having a fund-raiser to solicit funds for the Wood River program,

Amanda told her, contrary to stated policy, that Hoover CAC was not encouraging them this year. The policy council and Hoover CAC Head Start staff, in reviewing requirements such as the multipart parent education topics offered during the 1993–94 year, might consider the impact of such policies upon the autonomy of local committees.

Responding to Changing Family Demographics

The most visible sign of parent involvement at Wood River was volunteering. Parents volunteered in the classroom, for field trips, and to fill in for vacationing or ill staff. However, volunteer hours at Wood River, like at most other Head Start programs, have decreased in response to the growing number of parents who work outside the home. Currently most Head Start children, like the majority of preschool children in this country, spend a portion of each day in child care. At Wood River over half of the children were delivered to a day care center or licensed day care home after Head Start. In recognition of this change in family demographics, the *Advisory Committee Report on Head Start Quality and Expansion* (U.S. DHHS, 1993a) stated that "Head Start can no longer continue to be a half day program for children in those families that need full day full year services" (p. 47). Although Hoover CAC did not offer full day care options for parents, other Head Start grantees in the state were offering such services.

Judy explained that she did not want to work 40 hours per week, year round, as day care teachers commonly do. She enjoyed having her summers free. Susan, on the other hand, welcomed the possibility of full-time, full-year work. She had previous experience as a day care teacher and would be able to give up her part-time positions at the drug store and the community education program should she be offered full-time work with benefits.

Though Hoover CAC has received increases in Head Start funding, the policy has been to increase teachers' preparation time and in-service training instead of extending the children's program day or year. Judy told me that she thinks that teachers have too much preparation time at this point and that it would be best to cut back on the amount of this and on the length of the in-service training at the start of the year.

As I listened to Judy and Susan talk about their different viewpoints about extending Head Start services from part to full day, I recognized that their positions were based upon their work history, changes in Hoover CAC policy, and their understanding of the Wood River Head Start families. Judy, acknowledging that many families needed full-time care, stated that the present Head Start year suited her needs. Susan, who had taught in a day care center and presently worked two jobs to support her family, would prefer a full-day, full-year program. Judy and Susan's responses show how individual history and needs shape how staff interpret potential changes in policy.

At the beginning of the school year the staff got to know the children and families. As the staff became acquainted with the children, they figured out how to handle individual problems. During my first year at Wood River, one boy, Mark, vocalized his strong dislike of foods. As staff and children listened to his complaints, we labeled him a finicky eater. In the following story, I describe Mark, and how, over time, the staff developed a local policy in response to his eating pattern.

6

Developing Policies from Practice: The Story of Mark, the Finicky Eater

AIR FERNS

I thought about air ferns as I sat across the lunch table from Mark, a red-haired 3-year-old, who had a runny nose. "Go and get a Kleenex," I told him. He got off the bench and went to the end of the table, rubbing a Kleenex under his nose. The food was laid out in bowls and on plates, ready for the children to pass it down, family style.

Mark looked at me: "I'm not gonna eat it."

"Come on, Mark, give it a try," I said.

"No, I'm not gonna try it."

"Okay, but put a bit on your plate, and pass it on; you have to have some on your plate," I told him.

He dished himself out three peas and handed the dish on. Then came the buttered bread; he plopped a slice on his plate, beside the three peas. As the food was passed, he added a meat patty, green jello, and a pickle slice. He sat and looked at the food on his plate, picked up his milk glass and drained it. A white mustache outlined his mouth.

"I'm done," he told me, "I wanna clear off my plate."

"You'll have to wait a few minutes until some of the other children are done. How about trying the jello?" I asked.

"I'm not eating it; my mother is making me food at home," he told me.

"What is she making you?" I asked.

"French fries and fish sticks; she is making me French fries and fish sticks," he said, as though they were the only thing he would eat.

Judy looked down at Mark's plate. "Mark, I want you to try that patty; take a bite of it." Judy leaned over and cut a thin slice for him.

Mark looked at the slice and moved it around with his fork. As the children started to finish eating, he picked up his plate and scraped the meat patty, three peas, buttered bread, green jello, and pickle into the trash. He put his silverware and cup in a plastic dish pan. He started to run around the gym, and other kids joined in the chase.

"Come back here!" yelled Judy, "I didn't tell you that you could run around. Now you just sit down here and wait." The kids grew restless waiting for the adults to finish.

"Okay," said Judy "you can run and chase." As the kids started to run, Judy, Susan, and I sat at the table, finishing up our plates.

"You know," I told Judy and Susan, "Mark reminds me of these ferns my sister told me about, that live on air. The funny thing is that I never saw Paula water these things. One day I asked her, 'How do you keep those things alive?' She laughed, 'You just let them go until they really are dry, then add some water.' "

The next day at lunch, Mark sat next to Susan, passing the roast pork on without taking any.

"Hey," said Philip, one of the children, "You have to take some. Put some on your plate."

Mark took the bowl back and picked out a small piece of pork.

Susan pointed to the roast pork, buttered bread, mixed vegetables, and pear slice on Mark's plate: "Mark, I want you to take a bite of these things."

Mark ate his pear slice and asked for more.

Susan replied, "First eat some of your other food, then you can have some more."

The children from the special education program were in the gym, doing exercises at the far end, lying on mats, lifting their legs up and down to the teacher's count, "One and up and two and up and three and up." Mark looked underneath the table and kicked his leg.

Susan told him, "If you want some more pears, you have to eat some other food."

Mark replied, "My mother is cooking for me at home."

Judy added, "If you don't eat, you can't have an ice cream bar."

"I don't like those anyway," Mark told her, continuing to kick, and peeking under the table.

At our table, Judy was looking through the roast pork dish, picking out the pieces without fat to put on her plate. I passed the bread by—too much butter to my liking—but loaded up on the roast pork, fat and all. Judy picked out a few carrots to put on her plate, passing up the peas. The children finished scraping their plates. Judy got the ice cream bars and started to pass them out.

"Can't have one today," she told Mark, who was sitting next to the wall.

"I don't like them anyway," he responded, kicking his feet on the floor.

On the third day, Mark was back at the table near Judy and me.

Judy said, "Today, Mark, if you don't eat, you can't have a cookie."

We started to pass the food down the table: hot dogs, rolls, beans, sauerkraut. I looked at the hot dogs, bright red and rubbery. Perhaps I could skip those, I thought to myself. I took a roll and passed them on to Mark, who took one and put in on his plate. Next came the sauerkraut. I took a large portion and scooped a few pale stands onto Mark's plate. Then came the hot dogs. Four-year-old Ben had the tongs and put one in his roll. I fluffed up my roll, hoping that nobody would see it was empty. I handed the dogs on to Mark.

Ben said, "He doesn't have one."

I looked at Ben, and then around the room, knowing that he was talking about me. Ben had some trouble with pronoun use. "He doesn't have one," he repeated, pointing to my plate. Ben told me, "You have to have one, even if you don't eat it."

Judy smiled at me. She got away with just a roll on her plate, and I got caught in the act. I took a hot dog and put it in my bun. Yuck, I said to myself, and went to the kitchen to get some mustard to put on it. Mark took a hot dog and passed on the bowl. He ate his hot dog, leaving little on his plate aside from the few pale strands of sauerkraut. Then he went to scrape his plate, rubbing the rubber spatula against the sauerkraut, pushing it into the trash.

I waited for the children to finish, placed my napkin over the hot dog, and pushed it into the trash. Judy went for the cookies and handed them out, "Here you go, Mark; want one, Deb?"

I took the chocolate chip cookie and sat to eat it.

"These are good," said Mark crunching on his cookie. "Just like the ones my mother makes."

EATING POLICIES

During my first lunch at Head Start I learned about the policy requiring staff and children to serve themselves a portion of all foods. This local practice originates from the Hoover CAC Meal Evaluation Form, dated July 1991, which states that all children are to be "given all the required food components." In compliance with Head Start Performance Standards, all Hoover CAC center-based Head Start programs prepared a child-sized serving of each food and beverage for daily snacks and lunches. The Wood River staff instruct children to serve themselves a portion of each food. At first children balked when told to put foods they disliked on their plates. For instance, 3-year-old Thomas put one strand of spinach on his plate and then passed the bowl on. He then pushed the spinach from his plate to the table.

When children such as Thomas complained that they did not like a food, or were "not going to eat it," a staff member or child reminded, "You don't have to eat it, you just have to put it on your plate." The children grow accustomed to serving themselves portions of every food and then throwing away those foods they do not like.

Every day Wood River staff threw away sizable quantities of food because federal policy forbade programs from reheating leftovers or giving the food away. Judy felt that the main reason that the program threw away so much food was the Hoover CAC Head Start lunch menu. Hoover CAC, which also operated the senior citizen dining program, served most Head Start programs the senior citizen dining menu. This menu included foods described in the story, including roast beef, pork patties, chicken à la king, canned vegetables, bread, butter, canned fruit, and milk. Judy made several requests to Hoover CAC to change from the senior citizen's menu to the school lunch menu, thinking that children were more likely to eat foods on the school lunch menu, which included hot dogs, fish sticks, pizza, and tacos. Because the same personnel prepared both the school and senior citizen's lunches, the change would not require any additional arrangements. Judy received permission to request a school lunch menu occasionally but not on a regular basis.

Perhaps in response to the concern about wasted food, in 1993 the U.S. Department of Agriculture, which sets policies for school lunch programs, changed the long-standing policy requiring that children be served a specified amount of food. Federal policy still required that staff prepare the same amount of food, but now children could choose which foods to put on their plates. The updated Hoover CAC Head Start policies and procedures manual, distributed to all programs, contained a copy of this new meal pattern policy. However, the Wood River staff, like most Head Start staff, did not read the manual. Ann Norstrom, the Head Start director, told me about this change in policy and her decision not to tell staff about it. She wanted staff to continue encouraging children to eat new foods and felt that if staff knew of the policy change they might alter their practices.

The Wood River staff, in a decision based upon their working knowledge of Hoover CAC policies, continued to require children to put a portion of each food on their plate and encouraged them to try all foods served. This tasting policy is based upon the Performance Standards, which state, "Food is not used as a punishment or reward, and . . . children are encouraged but not forced to eat or taste" (U.S. DHHS, 1992, p. 44). During on-site visits, Hoover CAC administrators complete the Meal Evaluation Form, which asks, "Are efforts made to encourage consumption of the minimum portion requirements?"

Staff encouraged children sitting near them to try new foods. After observing a staff member eat an unfamiliar food, some children would taste it. Children, like the Wood River staff, varied in how much they consumed and the foods they liked. Judy picked out trimmed pieces of meat, I tried to avoid hot dogs, and Mark liked French fries and fish sticks.

DEFINING MARK AS A FINICKY EATER

During morning snack, served shortly after his arrival at 10 A.M., Mark usually ate all his food. He especially liked waffles and fruit. At lunch, served at

11:45 A.M., he ate the foods he liked, drank his milk, and told the staff when he was done. There were other children who ate little during lunch, including Bonnie and June. Bonnie was a very quiet child who complied with the requirement to put all food items on her plate. She waited patiently for the end of the meal and then scraped most of the food into the trash. June, more vocal than Bonnie, would occasionally tell staff that she was not going to eat the foods served. However, unlike Mark, she was not consistent or loud about her food dislikes, and generally she was allowed to eat what she wanted.

Each lunchtime with Mark was unique in some ways: He sat next to different children and staff, his appetite fluctuated, and the menu varied. Unique as the individual lunch experiences were, staff, over the course of many different lunches, began to define Mark as a finicky eater. This process began when staff commented on the interactions they had with Mark during lunchtime. If Susan sat next to Mark at lunch, she might mention to me after the meal that he only ate his pears and drank his milk. Later in the week, Ruth, after sitting next to Mark, might comment that he told her that he "wasn't going to eat anything." It was through this process of ad hoc, informal networking that staff began to define Mark as a finicky eater.

Staff consensus about Mark's eating habits developed during September and October as they assembled "observations from actual moments and situations dispersed over time [and] organiz[ed] them . . . in accordance with the 'instructions' that the concept provides" (Smith, 1990, p. 15). For staff, the meaning of "Mark, the finicky eater," was located in the daily lunch encounters. He was not always a finicky eater, but he was the most vocal of the children about his food preferences. Regardless of our individual beliefs about how to handle children's eating patterns, we agreed that he was a finicky eater.

Although we never referred to Mark as a finicky eater in front of the other children, they were aware of our daily encounters with him, as was evident in a conversation that occurred between Jasmine and Mark at lunch in December. Jasmine asked him, "Do you want Santa to come? You have to eat that food on your plate all gone. He is watching and he won't bring you presents if you don't eat."

Mark responded, "He is going to bring me presents."

Jasmine said, "Not if you don't eat, he won't."

Mark retorted, "Yes, he will."

Staff tried various approaches to dealing with Mark, and during the first few months of the program, there was no consensus on how to handle his eating. I tended to ignore his comments. Judy told him he would need to try foods before he could have dessert. Susan favored withholding seconds on a favorite food unless he tried a bite of a new food. Ruth and Judy reminded him several times to try other foods. Mark responded to these approaches by crying, saying that he did not like the dessert, and telling us that he would vomit if he tried a new food. This last tactic was successful, due in part to Judy's previous history as an assistant teacher and her negative memory of cleaning up after sick children. However, in January Judy decided that it was time for Mark to try new foods.

DEVELOPING A POLICY FROM PRACTICE

In early January, Judy told Mark that he had to stay at the table until he tried his potatoes. Judy described the meal:

> Yesterday Mark ate a bit of potatoes and meat. I told him that if he didn't eat, he couldn't go outside to sled. He put the potatoes in his mouth and looked like he was going to gag. I told him, "If you gag and throw up, you can't go outside either." He chewed it and then I gave him a piece of meat. Later when he came back to the room, he told Susan that I had given him some more meat and that he drank his milk too.

Judy explained that she thought it was important for Mark to have a "bite of protein" every day. The day that Judy had implemented this "bite-of-protein" policy, I had been working at another Head Start program. When she first told me about this policy, I felt a knot in my stomach. Just the day before, when she had asked me what I thought about Mark and his eating, I had suggested that she encourage him to try new foods, withhold seconds on favorite foods until he tasted a new food, and ignore his complaints. I had given her an article on fussy eating that I had found in a book available to Head Start parents.

Personal Experiences and Policy

Judy and I had talked several times about our own children and their eating patterns. My son, James, was a fussy eater who, gradually over time, outgrew this behavior. When James was Mark's age, my husband and I had brought him to the doctor, who assured us that James was healthy and that we should continue offering him healthy food choices. Judy shared that she had often ignored her own sons' fussy eating habits. I thought that Judy and I agreed in our approach to handling finicky eaters, but when she announced her new policy, I realized that we had different perceptions of how to work with Mark.

Uncertain how to respond to Judy's new food policy at Head Start, I called my graduate advisor, Daniel Walsh. Daniel told me a story about a

finicky eater in one of his classrooms and how he developed an eating policy
for the boy, whose ill health he described, attributing this to poor diet. Daniel
ate lunch with the boy every day in the classroom. At first the child vomited
his meal, but gradually over time, he learned to eat his food and grew health-
ier. Looking back on this, Daniel told me that he still thought this policy best
for this boy and Daniel challenged me to rethink the early childhood literature, including the article on fussy eating I had given Judy. He said:

> As a teacher, I always associated best practices with those pristinely dressed
> middle-aged women, back before I was middle aged myself, who came into my
> classroom and made announcements about what was good or bad and then went
> back to their offices away from the daily struggles I was having and my own
> negotiations of certain glaring realities, e.g., no matter how effective I was, I
> knew that the kids' lives were pretty weighted against them. (personal communi-
> cation, January 4, 1994)

Daniel's comment highlighted how values and past personal and professional experiences are keys to understanding how I and the other members
of the Wood River staff reacted to Mark. The issue was not embedded in the
nutrition literature that Daniel referred to as best practices, but in staff's
understanding of the problem. Daniel, like Judy, justified the short period of
discomfort for the child in terms of the long-term health outcome. As I told
Judy, I would have allowed Mark to complain at the meal and restrict seconds
on his favorite foods until he tried a new food. However, I decided that in my
dual position as researcher/volunteer I would follow the new mealtime plan.
I felt that if I pressed the issue with Judy or discussed the situation with
Hoover CAC administrators I would be overstepping my role as a volunteer
in the program and violating the trust I had established with Judy.

The bite-of-protein practice operated at the local level in much the same
way that an official policy did. When I described the situation to my husband,
John, fishing for words to describe how staff developed this practice and its
relationship to eating policies, he said, "You aren't talking about policies *and*
practice. You are talking about policies *from* practice." It was his insight that
led me to understand that the Wood River staff was developing local policies,
which I then called "policies from practice," based upon their interpretations
of official policies and the daily realities of working at Wood River and serving the families and children.

Implementing the Bite-of-Protein Policy

During January and February, a staff member, usually Judy, sat with Mark
and cut a small portion of "protein" for him to taste. At first Mark cried and

gagged and occasionally vomited. Each staff member developed a different way to handle the bite-of-protein policy. Judy reminded Mark verbally several times that he had to taste the food. Susan told him once and held out a spoon with a small piece of meat on it. I often held his hand while he chewed his food and sent stickers and notes home telling his mother what he had tasted at lunch.

Shortly after Judy established the bite-of-protein policy from practice, Amanda Red scheduled a home visit with Mark's mother, Karen. Karen explained that Mark was a finicky eater at home and that she had a difficult time getting him to try new foods. She asked Amanda to have Judy send her a list of the foods he tried at school. Judy spoke with Karen about Mark's eating and told her that "he is tasting foods. Some days he gags, but not too much."

Karen shared that she had tried this approach at home, but Mark had cried and thrown up. Judy told her that "he did that for a while here too. Then it got better."

When Andrea Holland, the Hoover CAC dietitian, visited in February, Judy pointed Mark out during lunch and said, "He is hardly eating anything. I know I shouldn't be doing this, but I tell him he has to have one bite of protein every day. He gags a bit, but he gets it down. He just eats French fries and fish sticks at home."

Andrea asked, "Does he eat any foods here?"

Judy replied, "French fries and fish sticks and fruit."

Andrea suggested, "Have you tried doing some food activities to get him interested in trying some different foods?"

Judy told her, "We had them help with the pizza and the pigs in a blanket." (The latter is a hot dog rolled in a crescent roll and baked.)

Judy turned to Susan and me, "Did he eat the hot dog?"

I said, "I think so." Susan and I told Judy and Andrea that we could not remember if he ate the pizza.

Andrea concluded, "Well, he must be getting enough foods to make it on."

Judy then suggested to Andrea again that the Head Start menu be changed from the senior citizen's to the school lunch menu. She told Andrea that the children were more likely to eat the foods served to school-aged children. For instance, hot dogs, a food that Mark enjoyed, were never served on the senior citizen's menu but were served on the school lunch menu. Andrea answered that she was concerned about the fat content in the school lunch menus and that she thought it was important that the Head Start children try the foods on the senior citizen's menu. Judy persisted for 2 years in trying to change the menu, and for a brief period of several weeks, the Hoover CAC Head Start administration approved the change. However, this was not long lasting, and Wood River once again served the senior citizen's meals.

Staff continued to enforce the bite-of-protein policy. At the end of February, Susan reported at the Wood River staff meeting that Mark was eating bites of food on his own. In April, Mark entered the lunchroom and announced, "I am going to taste my spaghetti and bread." Mark continued to try foods on his own, sampling most of the items on his plate. As he began to eat foods on his own and complained less, staff complimented him on his eating.

EXAMINING POLICY IMPLICATIONS

Eating Policy as a Relationship Idea

In "Air Ferns" I depicted three Head Start eating policies: encouraging children to taste new foods, having children serve themselves a portion of each food offered, and not forcing children to eat. These three policies promote different understandings of what it means to eat at Head Start. One interpretation is that young children attending Head Start must serve themselves foods they do not like. The staff encourages, but does not force, children to try these new foods. These children and staff then throw away the food they do not eat. These policies resulted in such practices as teachers and children reminding each other, "Remember, you have to put it on your plate, but you don't have to eat it," and staff disposing of large quantities of food every day.

When Judy defined the bite-of-protein policy from practice, she let Mark know that it was important for him to try new foods at Head Start. Judy, when talking with Andrea, acknowledged that she was operating outside sanctioned practices by "forcing" Mark to eat, and at the same time, acknowledged the value of her goal, getting Mark to try different kinds of foods.

From her personal values and working knowledge of Mark and his eating pattern, Judy believed that her policy was in Mark's best interest. In Pauly's (1991) words, the eating policy was a relationship idea. Pauly describes how teachers and students develop relationship ideas by observing and interacting with one another, always aware of their relationships with others. As teachers watch, observe, and interact with children, they determine how they can best interact with groups of children and individuals. As Pauly states:

> The link between . . . relationships and the search for solutions has an important
> result. It ties each classroom's way of teaching and learning to relationships that
> have been adopted in that particular classroom. (p. 88)

Judy developed the bite-of-protein policy from practice only after we had
observed and eaten many lunches with Mark. The policy from practice resulted from our many interchanges with Mark and from Judy's conclusion
that other tactics were not effective in encouraging him to try other foods.

Judy, my advisor, Daniel, and other early care and education teachers
with whom I have discussed mealtimes argue that a tasting policy is critical
for children such as Mark. Once such a policy is initiated, children often start
eating foods on their own. The teacher has established a mandate with which
the child is expected to comply. My limited attempts using this approach
have led to some children trying new foods, others sitting at the table for long
periods, and still others vomiting. If children tried the food, the policy
worked fine. However, for those children who sat at the table for long periods
or vomited, the mealtime resulted in unpleasant consequences for both the
child and me. Perhaps I am, as Judy said, a "soft heart," but I did not have
the stamina or conviction to enforce the policy until the children started
eating foods on their own. These methods are incongruent with my beliefs
about eating and teaching children about eating. From my viewpoint, children should choose from healthy foods and enjoy the meal. From Daniel and
Judy's viewpoint, it was important for the child and teacher to work through
a short but difficult time that resulted in the child eating more food.

Judy told both Mark's mother, Karen, and Andrea about the bite-of-
protein policy. Karen, we learned, had tried to get Mark to eat different
foods, but just like at Wood River, he cried or vomited. Staff thought that
Karen allowed Mark to eat junk foods at home and that this affected his
eating pattern at school. Ruth reported that Mark often got on the bus with
candy or potato chips in his pocket and protested loudly when she told him
he could not eat them on the bus. Karen asked for a list of foods that Mark
ate at school in the hope that she could get him to eat those foods at home.
We never learned if his home eating pattern changed.

Responsiveness of Administrators

Andrea's responses to Judy included questions about what Mark ate and her
conclusion that his food intake must be adequate for "him to make it on." In
this instance, Andrea did not ask staff if they had tried other approaches, nor
did she provide alternative strategies for staff to consider. Given my personal
feelings about the bite-of-protein policy, I was disappointed by Andrea's response because I hoped that she could give us insight into Mark's eating

style. Yet when I placed Andrea's response in the context of the interchanges we had with other Hoover CAC coordinators and managers over the year, the comments took on a familiar pattern. Because administrators were removed from the daily work of teachers and Head Start programs, they had a limited understanding of the program's history and complexity. Even had Andrea sat beside Mark, she would not have understood what it was like to sit beside him day after day and listen to him complain about the food. By the time Andrea visited in February, Mark had started to eat foods on his own, and he rarely complained.

Though Andrea briefly discussed Mark's eating pattern with the staff and suggested that his food intake was sufficient, the main focus of her visit was to monitor and evaluate program operations to ensure that Wood River complied with the Performance Standards and Hoover CAC policies. Just as staff completed paperwork as a procedural matter to comply with prescriptive policies, Andrea inspected the kitchen and mealtime procedures and completed evaluation forms to measure how well the program staff complied with health and nutrition policies.

In my listening to Andrea, the policies that seemed most important were related to food service issues, including food temperature, kitchen sanitation, and equipment. Andrea noted that the gym tables and benches, designed for older school-aged children, were too big for the Head Start children. Dating back to the 1960s and in poor working condition, they folded into the gym wall and required two teachers and a crowbar to take down and put up. Despite our efforts to shorten the distance from the tables to the benches by tying them together, many children seated at the benches were too far from the tables and could not see over them. However, Andrea's concern about the tables did not result in Hoover CAC purchasing new furniture, and we continued to eat at the same tables and benches.

The ongoing conversation between Judy, Andrea, and the Hoover CAC health component manager about the lunch menu highlights how limited staff's decision-making power was in making changes about the daily operation of the program. To the Wood River staff, the switch made sense because children would eat more food, resulting in less waste. It was hard to understand why Hoover CAC did not approve this request. Yet there may have been valid administrative reasons why Hoover CAC decided to serve the senior citizen lunch menu, but aside from a comment from Andrea about fat content, the rationale was not explained to me or the other staff.

In the same way that administrators lack knowledge of the daily operation of programs such as Wood River, local Head Start program staff had limited interest in and understanding of Head Start and Hoover CAC policies, policy implementation, and changes in policies. As Johnson (1994) wrote:

> Most teachers think of educational policy as a nuisance or a threat, devised by "Them"—the policy makers who work in the Central Office, the State House, or Washington—to control the work of "Us"—the people who really know kids and classrooms. Though new policies often bring with them money to fund worthy programs, they inevitably carry new obligations and restrictions, many of which, teachers believe, are misguided and interfere with good schooling. (p. 15)

To us at Wood River, the policy making and resulting rules and regulations seemed restrictive and often misguided and made it difficult for us to choose the best options for the children and families.

One remedy for the misunderstandings between Head Start staff and administrators is to find ways for the groups to share more about their concerns, problems, and solutions to problems. For instance, during the discussion about Mark, Andrea could have inquired about how the problem began and what strategies staff had tried with him. When talking about the lunch menu, Andrea might have provided more information about why the senior citizen menu was a better choice for Head Start. Perhaps Hoover CAC could have agreed to a trial run with the school lunch menu to find out if the children ate more food. These conversations may have promoted better communication between Wood River and Hoover CAC Head Start administrators and led to creative solutions to remedy local problems.

Although Judy was aware that the bite-of-protein policy was in conflict with stated Hoover CAC meal policies, she believed that it was important for Mark to learn to eat other foods. The staff distinguished between the official eating policies and the working policy of eating with Mark every day. This distinction between official and working policies is highlighted in the following story, "Empty Hands on the Bus."

7

Official Policies and Working Policies

EMPTY HANDS ON THE BUS

I didn't have a clue about "riding the bus" before I joined the Wood River staff, but I had conducted a training session for Hoover CAC bus drivers and riders. In August 1993, we discussed different ways of handling disruptive bus behavior. I brought along with me puppets and stories, demonstrated how the bus riders might use them with the children, and handed out packets with words and music for familiar songs and finger-plays to each of the riders. I recall that the bus drivers and riders were cordial and polite.

It wasn't until Ruth called and asked me to substitute for her that I learned about riding the bus. Two weeks after I started volunteering at Wood River, she called because her son was ill and she needed to get him to the doctor. I said, "Sure," and Gary came by at around 9 A.M. to pick me up for the first route. When I got on the bus, Gary explained his job and mine. "I drive the bus; you make sure the kids are safe."

He described the daily routine. "Ruth greets each child as they get on the bus. They put the backpacks in that basket." Gary pointed to a laundry basket behind his seat. "Then she gets them seated and helps with the car seat or seat belt. You sit with the child and visit until the next one gets on."

I thought, No problem, and Gary and I drove off. At the first stop we picked up Caleb. We said good morning to his mother. Gary, as is his custom, asked Caleb what he had had for breakfast. Caleb put his backpack in the basket, sat down, and buckled his seat belt. He and I chatted until we reached Philip's trailer. Caleb, who always had a belt four sizes too large for him, tightened it as he told me about playing ball with his dad.

We repeated the greeting and getting-on-the-bus routine, and Philip settled into his seat. All proceeded smoothly until we traveled a narrow, winding river road to pick up Jasmine, our fourth passenger. By the time we reached Jasmine's my stomach was upset, and I realized I was getting carsick. The trips up and down the aisle became more difficult with each stop.

During the rest of the trip, I followed the routine and at Gary's suggestion read a story and sang songs with the children. When we arrived at Wood River, I helped the children off the bus, took an aspirin, chewed an antacid, and gulped down some fresh air. After a brief stop at Wood River, Gary and I headed out to Hudson for the second group of children. We traveled from house to house picking up the children. Sarah got on the bus with some magazines to donate to the program, and during the ride back to Wood River, the children and I took turns looking through the pictures.

Shortly before 11 A.M. we drove into the Early Learning Center parking lot. After dropping off the children and me, Gary headed over to pick up the lunches from the school cafeteria in Starr. By 12:30 he and I were back in the bus again, bringing children from the first route home.

In January 1994, 4 months after my first bus ride, Hoover CAC asked me to conduct another training session for the bus riders and drivers. By this time I had substituted for Ruth on several occasions and had dealt with many types of disruptive behavior, including children who did not want to buckle their seat belts, children who took their seat belts off, children who yelled, children who cried, children who lost things on the bus, children who hit each other, children who did not want to get on the bus, and children who did not want to get off the bus. I realized that this job was much tougher than I had first imagined.

I asked Ruth and Gary for suggestions on what I should talk about during the training. Ruth had told me that she'd heard that the children weren't supposed to have anything in their hands during the hour-long bus ride to and from the center. Ruth asked what she was supposed to do with the children on the bus if they couldn't have playthings. She said that the kids got fidgety and couldn't just sit there staring out the window. After my few bus trips, I too wondered how you keep children occupied through four bus routes of an hour each.

When the Hoover CAC Head Start transportation component manager called to discuss topics for the in-service, I asked for clarification on the "empty-hands-on-the-bus" policy. She checked on it and later called to explain that the policy was established to prevent child injury in case of a sudden stop or accident. She said that the bus riders, like Ruth, could sing and read books to keep the children occupied. I don't know about Ruth, but after the morning route my singing and story voice was worn out. I thought about using music and story tapes but the tape recorder in the bus was broken.

One day Ruth and I were talking about the empty-hands-on-the-bus policy. Judy joined our discussion and listened as we described the policy and its rationale. She then said to Ruth and me, "Who is making these policies, anyway? Are they the people who are riding the bus? I will tell you what I think. I think that it should be up to the bus driver and rider. They should make the decision. If it works for them, then it is okay."

Judy's response captures well the difference that she saw between workable solutions to riding the bus and the mandates from Hoover CAC administrators, who did not deal with the daily realities of operating the program. Gary noted that the policy makers at Hoover CAC had little understanding of the day-to-day realities of riding the bus. He suggested that instead of coming out and monitoring staff, the administrators should come and spend some "real time" riding the bus for a few days to get a feel for what it is like. Despite the official empty-hands policy, Judy also shared that she knew that many of the bus riders in other Hoover CAC Head Start programs did bring things for the children to play with on the bus. She said that one rider in a nearby program had small toy trucks and cars for the children to play with.

When I conducted the bus driver and rider training, the Hoover CAC administrators reviewed their policy. Ruth, like other bus riders, did not question the policy in front of the administrators. However, on a daily basis, she decided what the children would do on the bus rides. Some days she had magazines for the children to look at and other times stuffed animals to hold.

NEED FOR OFFICIAL POLICIES

Despite the belief held by staff that many policies were not applicable to realities at Wood River, they did not dispute the need for policies per se. Gary described Head Start transportation policies and how these policies had changed over time. He said that 6 years ago, when he first took the job, there "weren't any policies at all." At that time Gary drove a van, and all the children were picked up in one route. The van didn't have enough seat belts for all the children. Those who weren't seat belted sat on the van floor.

Hoover CAC Head Start then relied on parents to volunteer as van riders. The bus route changed daily to accommodate the parent who was the rider for that particular day. When a parent wasn't able to meet their riding obligation, Gary would ask the parent next on the route if he or she could ride for that day. If Gary couldn't find a parent volunteer, he returned to the Head Start center and a staff member rode with him instead.

If parents were not there when Gary brought their children home, he drove the child to his house and then tried to reach the parent. Sometimes children spent several hours at Gary's until the parents came to pick the children up.

Gary was "fed up" with the lack of policy. He and other bus riders met with Ann Norstrom, the Head Start director, and the transportation component manager, Nora Jacobs. Nora's position has since changed and she now works as the home-based education component manager. The bus drivers and Head Start administrators developed a set of bus policies that included seat belt regulations, a nonsmoking policy, drop-off and pick-up procedures for parents and children, and bus safety rules. During this time the Wood

River Head Start program changed from one bus route to two. Gary said that the bus policies were important and that most parents followed them well.

LEARNING ABOUT HEAD START POLICIES

Judy and other staff usually did not distinguish between the various layers of policy—federal, state, or agency—but referred to policy as Hoover CAC policy. There are several reasons that staff probably referred to all policies this way. First, as Gary recalled, there was a time when there were few policies governing bus driving and other areas of the program. Until Ann became the Head Start director, there was no Head Start policies and procedures manual; it was under her direction that the manual was developed. It included the Hoover CAC personnel policies, education, parent involvement, social services, transportation and health policies, the Head Start Performance Standards, and programmatic and attendance forms. Each program had a copy of the manual in a large notebook. At the end of each school year, the manual was returned to Hoover CAC for updating of policies and forms.

The second reason staff referred to all policies as Hoover CAC policies is that they often learned about policy through discussions among themselves and from Hoover CAC administrators. Susan, Judy, and Gary explained Head Start policies to Ruth and me, as newcomers, in the context of the daily events at the program. I learned how the required curriculum topics are incorporated into weekly lesson plans by helping Susan plan for the upcoming week's activities. Ruth learned bus-riding policies through discussions with Judy and Gary. Every month, as required by Hoover CAC, Judy conducted team meetings for the Wood River Head Start staff. During these meetings, staff discussed policy-related issues such as the empty-hands-on-the-bus policy and sharing space with the other programs at the Early Learning Center.

During 1993–94, Hoover CAC Head Start teaching staff attended 13 days, and bus drivers and site aides 7 days, of training and workshops. Ruth, who attended a special orientation session for new employees and the 7 scheduled days of training, stated that she had never been through so much training in her life. A Head Start administrator, who was a former Head Start teacher, stated that when administrators spent so much time during orientations and training focusing on paperwork, they gave the staff a message about what was important.

During preservice training at the beginning of the year, Head Start administrators reviewed policy changes and distributed revised copies of the policy manual to all site managers. At Wood River the manual was kept at the bottom of a closet, inaccessible to anyone wishing to consult it. One day a kindergarten teacher asked Susan for a list of Head Start children entering kindergarten the following fall. Judy was on vacation, and Susan asked me whether we should do this. I suggested that we consult the policies and procedures manual. We worked together to get the manual out of the closet, but after looking through it, could not locate the information. Susan then called Martha Calle, the center-based education component manager, who first told her that she could release the names and then called and said that she could not. When Amanda Red, the family advocate, visited later that day, Susan related the kindergarten teacher's request. Amanda showed us a form signed by parents that was in each child's folder giving permission for Head Start to release information to the public schools.

What I realized from this event and from my observations at Wood River is that staff learned about policies from talking with each other, asking staff in other Hoover CAC programs, attending Hoover CAC Head Start meetings, and calling the Hoover CAC office.

EMPHASIZING OR DOWNPLAYING POLICIES

Hoover CAC Head Start administrators emphasized certain policies when de-emphasizing others. For instance, Martha Calle knew about the policy prohibiting staff from wearing jeans to work but did not "make a big deal about it," because she thought it was important for staff to feel comfortable working with children. However, she noted that if the dress code policy was enforced in one center, she would likely be required to enforce it in all centers.

As pointed out in Chapter 6, Ann Norstrom did not tell staff about the change in the eating policy, which required children to serve themselves a portion of each food, to the new policy that stated that the foods simply had to be offered to each child. Ann explained, as was noted, that the reason she did not tell staff about this change is that she wanted them to continue to encourage children to try new foods. At Wood River, staff still continue to have children serve themselves a portion of each food despite their knowledge that the policy has changed. The official policy had changed, but the working policy remained the same. When the program dietitian, Andrea Holland, visited and ate lunch with the children and staff, she did not inform staff about the change in eating policy.

As I listened to the staff, I realized that the same policy could be defined differently depending upon the context and situation. For instance, one day Judy noted Allison King had four unexcused absences. Allison's mother and father were in the process of a divorce, and home–Head Start communication had suffered; her parents often did not call in to let staff know when Allison would be absent. The Hoover CAC Head Start *Parent Handbook* states that "if there are chronic attendance problems, your child's place may be filled by another child" (Hoover CAC, 1993, p. 28). Judy interpreted this to mean that Allison's unexcused absences might lead to her expulsion from the program. Judy told me, "I should report this, but I won't. She is going to stay in the program." Judy, by interpreting the policy in this way, signaled to the staff that in cases of family stress the needs of the children and family were considered more important than complying with an official policy.

Upon checking the absence policy, I found that it stated that an absence is excused when "the child's attendance is affected by temporary family situations" (Hoover CAC, 1993b, p. 28). Technically, Allison's absences could be classified as excused, and according to the policy, she would remain in the program.

Policies, then, are not uniformly interpreted or applied by either administrators or staff. Staff and administrators had different understandings of policies that may or may not have been congruent with written policies. Staff and administrators simultaneously maintained an understanding of the official policy and a workable policy. Martha Calle knew the official dress code policy prohibiting staff from wearing jeans, but her working policy was to ignore it when they did wear them. Likewise, Judy and Ruth knew the official policy prohibiting children from having anything in their hands during the bus ride, and at the same time Ruth, like many other Hoover CAC bus riders, developed a working policy allowing children to look at books or magazines during their ride to and from school.

EXAMINING POLICY IMPLICATIONS

In some instances the Wood River staff thought that official policies were unrealistic and developed working policies more suitable to the needs of the program. Though staff questioned Hoover CAC administrators' understanding of local conditions, they supported the development of policies to insure the safety of the children and staff.

In our daily interchanges, the Wood River staff discussed policies in a myriad of ways. Our positionality could change from one interchange to the next, depending upon the context, our mood, and the subject at hand. For example, when Ruth and I discussed the empty-hands-on-the-bus policy, Judy asked Ruth if she was "going to bring it up at the training." Ruth first responded that she was. Later she asked me if I thought she should bring it up. At the meeting, Ruth, like the other bus riders, listened unquestioningly to the description of the policy and why it was important. Positioned as a bus rider listening to her bosses, she did not choose to challenge an established policy, but in the context of the local program, she allowed the children to look at magazines on the bus. Staff's positionality is not unified, consistent, or easily measured. As in the empty-hands policy, Ruth viewed the policy differently depending upon the context of the interaction.

Judy and other staff voiced their disapproval of policies that they perceived as impeding their efforts to provide services to children and families. Staff viewed prescriptive policies, such as that of empty hands on the bus as signs of the distance between them and the administrative staff who, Gary suggested, should come and spend some "real time" riding the bus and helping out at the center.

The difference between how Wood River staff and Hoover CAC administrators interpreted policies was highlighted in implementing the official collaboration policy, which requires Hoover CAC grantees to work with other community-based early childhood programs. For the Hoover CAC administrators, this policy entailed negotiating a contract with the Wood River superintendent, monitoring the Wood River program and staff, and meeting occasionally with the Wood River school administrators and Head Start staff. For the Wood River staff, implementing the collaboration policy was a year-long process that began with moving the program from St. John's to the Early Learning Center. Implementing the policy entailed developing and maintaining relationships with the Early Learning Center staff and negotiating Head Start requirements with programs that operated under different policies and procedures. In the following chapter I examine the daily ramifications of implementing the collaboration policy and how staff developed collocation and collaboration practices to do so.

8

Developing Practices and Tiny Tales of Success

THE BLUE TARP

To start off, I came out well on this one. Judy and I had a running 50-cent bet over when the divider in the gym would be put up. She told me it would be done "right after Christmas break." I told her to dream on; it wouldn't be done by then. My prediction panned out: Sure enough, we came back from Christmas vacation, no divider was up, and it was almost 3 weeks later before it happened. Judy didn't make good on the bet right away. It was at lunch one day when we were talking to Grace, the gym teacher, that I mentioned that Judy and I had a bet going.

"We didn't bet money?" asked Judy.

"Yes, we did, 50 cents, so pay up," I told her.

After lunch, Judy handed me the money.

Judy stood by the wall showing me how to operate the divider. You pressed a button, and the tarp either came down or rolled back up.

"How much did it cost?" I asked.

"I think $2,500 or $2,800, I can't remember," said Judy.

"You and I are in the wrong business," I said. "We could have strung up something for less than that."

A few days later I asked Ann Norstrom, the Head Start director, about the divider, noting that "$2,800 is a lot of money."

"Well, it ended up costing more than that, considerably more, maybe closer to $4,000," responded Ann.

So the next day I went back to the school to survey the divider again: two large pieces of bright blue plastic tarp strung across the middle of the gym. The pieces had that new plastic smell, like a child's doll just out of the package. When I pressed the button, the tarp rolled up at the top of the gym ceiling.

One day, Susan, Judy, and I were watching the tarp lower. Susan said, "Did you notice that—large creases. Maybe we should leave it down to hang straight overnight." She went and checked with the janitor, Donna, who said that it needed to be up.

Even before the tarp came, Head Start ate snacks and lunch and did art projects at one end of the gym, using the tables that folded into the wall. Grace, the gym teacher, held classes for the special education children at the other end of the gym.

This gym sharing started in September, as part of the agreement that was worked out to accommodate Head Start's move to the Early Learning Center. Before the school year began, we were told that a divider would be put up in the gym. In October Judy wrote to the Head Start office and told them that the divider wasn't up yet. Later in the month, the county coordinator, Martha, came for a visit and said, "I can't believe that they don't have it up yet." In November, Judy complained, "I don't know why the people in the office don't take care of this. If they had to work this way just one day, just one day, it would get up real fast." Donna told us in December that if the divider wasn't up after Christmas, the school district was going to "call and get someone else to do it."

So at 10:10 each day we ate snack in the gym with our first group of children. They sat down at the tables and started to pass along a bowl of fruit and some crackers. There were plates, napkins, and glasses of milk set out in front of them. I sat across from Philip, and he told me what he did last night. "I got to watch this pay-for-view movie last night. It was scary to watch."

Jasmine asked, "Were there witches?"

Just then Grace started up her class at the other end of the gym. "All right, you guys, I want everyone to be over here by the blue mat." Grace's voice boomed, the way all gym teachers' and coaches' do. "Now when I say go, I want you to run up to the other end of the gym. READY, SET, GO!" yelled Grace.

Philip and Jasmine turned around so that they could see the children running towards us. The children stopped running at the blue mat near our table.

"Good JOB" started Grace. "NOW this time when you go back to the mat I want you to hop. Does everyone know how to do that? Michelle, you come out here and show us how to do it."

Michelle went to the front of the group and did some hopping.

Grace boomed, "Excellent! Thank you, Michelle; let's give her a clap."

The children in the gym class clapped, and Jasmine, sitting across from me, joined in. Soon the gym children were at the opposite end again.

"You know," Judy told me, "Grace wants the divider put up so that she has most of the space. She wants to leave the circle in the middle the way it is so she doesn't have to move her colored X's. I told her that was fine, that we probably didn't need as much room as she does."

But Donna told us that the divider had to go up in the middle of the room, and some months later when Judy heard that, she said, "Well, that is only fair. Why should we just get a tiny space and she has the rest? She could move those colored X's; all she has to do is buy some tape and do them on the circle at the end. I would even help her do that if she wanted."

So the divider ended up in the middle of the gym.

Judy commented, "I really think this is going to help with the noise, don't you?"

"I'm not sure about that," I replied.

After a few days Grace told us, "It might not be doing anything for the noise, but it sure helps with the visuals. Before they put it up, my kids were so distracted. Now they can focus so much better."

The noise from the other side of the divider was intriguing. One day, after morning snack, Susan was playing a game on our side of the divider waiting for Grace to finish up and take our children over for their gym class. She had the children lined up on one end of the tarp, ready to cross over. Through the curtain we could hear 4-year-old Leah, a child with a visual disability, crying.

The Head Start children crowded near the tarp opening to see Leah. I peaked through the split in the middle of the tarp with Philip and Jasmine.

Philip asked, "What's she doing?"

"Throwing the ball," I told him.

Leah threw the ball twice. Grace and the two other special education teachers clapped, and so did we.

During our lunchtimes, we couldn't see the gym class anymore unless someone was at the edge of the tarp or standing in the middle gap. But we could hear. Today Grace was playing a country and western record, loud; she was teaching the kids to line dance. Garth Brooks's twang was heard from one end of the gym to the other.

Judy said, "I can't believe that she is trying to teach them line dancing. I don't think they should be doing that."

Jasmine smiled and rocked to the beat. I told Philip to pass the roast pork along, but he couldn't hear me.

"PHILIP!" I said, raising my voice, "PASS THE MEAT."

He took hold of the dish I held out to him, scooped a portion onto his plate, and passed it on to Jasmine. In 15 minutes, Grace's class was over, and the gym seemed strangely silent. The effort of competing with Garth Brooks had exhausted us, and aside from a few kids who were fooling around at the table, we sat and ate in relative silence. Ben and Caleb were the ones fooling around, and I told them to stop it or they would have to get up and scrape their plates.

They continued, so I told them to get up. Ben started to cry, "I don't want to." He sat at the table, sobbing. Caleb cleaned off his plate and sat back down. The rest of the children started to finish, using the rubber spatula to scrape the leftover food into the trash, and to mill around the gym. Soon they were chasing each other, screaming. Jasmine was lying on the floor near the gap in the middle of the blue tarp, looking into the other side.

The teachers tired of the noise. Judy and I got up to bring the children back to the room for tooth brushing. Before we left, Judy went over to the wall and pressed a button, "Hey watch this!"

The blue tarp started to ascend to the rollers above. I stood with the children, watching. The moment was serious, and I was tempted to raise my hand in salute.

What I remember most about the first year at Wood River is the noise level in the gym. The room sharing continued for the following 2 years, and, during one semester when the family education program held sessions in the shared classroom in both the mornings and afternoons, 2 days per week, we spent the majority of the day in the gym.

In moving to the Early Learning Center, the Wood River staff had to negotiate access to space and resources with the other programs. This negotiation process took the form of two practices. (Practices are routines and activities that embody a local interpretation of official policy.) In this case, staff developed practices in relationship to the official collaboration policy, which states:

> The Head Start agency shall take steps to coordinate with the local educational agency serving the community involved . . . including . . . establishing channels of communication between Head Start staff and their counterparts in the schools . . . to facilitate coordination of programs. (Head Start Act of 1994, § 9837)

The first practice that the staff developed was collocation, which involved changing the Head Start schedule, adjusting to the present situation at the Early Learning Center, and simultaneously pressing for a permanent location. The second practice was cooperative programming with the staff of the other programs at the Early Learning Center.

THE PRACTICE OF COLLOCATION

Collocation practices occurred at two levels—Hoover CAC and local programs. Ann Norstrom developed a practice of collocating Head Start programs with other early childhood programs. The intent of the collaboration policy and Ann's collocation practice was for Head Start staff to coordinate services with other community-based early childhood programs.

For Ann and the other Head Start administrators, the practice of collocation entailed negotiating a rental agreement with the school district to collocate Head Start at the Early Learning Center. At the local level, the practice of collocation entailed establishing and maintaining relationships with the staffs of the other programs at the Early Learning Center, negotiating use of the facilities, and operating Head Start in compliance with Hoover CAC policies.

Establishing and Maintaining Relationships

Judy and the other Head Start staff worked to establish and maintain friendly relationships with the other program staff at the Early Learning Center. Judy met with Fran Mark, the family education director, to decide how the classroom was arranged and checked with Fran during the year to make sure that the room arrangement was working. Fran requested Judy's help in soliciting children for a kindergarten readiness class, and Judy distributed information to parents.

However, it was clear from the beginning that the public school programs—special education, family education, and kindergarten—had priority status for facilities and scheduling. Head Start was scheduled for the gym during the times that special education held gym class because the kindergarten teachers decided that their playroom was off-limits to Head Start. Head Start had access to the shared classroom only when the family education program was not using it and had to rearrange the schedule any time that the program needed the classroom.

Arranging the Schedule

Judy rearranged the Head Start schedule around those of the other Early Learning Center programs. When Judy and Susan arrived at 8, they went to the classroom that Head Start shared with the family education program and got the art materials for the day's project. Try as they may, they often forgot items that we needed during the morning and had to enter the classroom when family education classes were in session. On one occasion, Susan asked me to go back to the room and get some paintbrushes. She told me, "I just hate to have to go back in there." I agreed with her.

When the first group of children arrived at 10:00, the staff brought them to the bathroom and then to the gym to eat snack. Just as we had finished eating and moved to the adjoining table for art, Grace Camp began her gym class. The noise level was at times deafening. Children had difficulty hearing teachers' directions for the art project and were easily distracted by the activity at the other end of the gym.

The second group of Head Start children arrived shortly before 11 and joined their classmates in the gym for class with Grace Camp. Following gym, they moved to the classroom for circle time and a brief free-play period. Everyone then washed their hands and returned to the gym for lunch, just in time for Grace Camp's second gym class of the day.

Judy described 1993–94 school year as "making do." When Martha Calle commented on how well Judy had adjusted to the shared arrangements, Judy commented, "What else can I do except make the best of it?" Toward the end of October, the days grew colder, and the heating system in the gym

failed. The staff and children did the best they could under these circumstances, but sometimes the gym was too cold to use. Fortunately, on those
occasions we were able to use another classroom.

At one point when the family education program was on a 2-week break,
Judy remarked, "The room is ours for 2 weeks and we can do whatever we
want!" This seemed like a luxury to us, to have the room to ourselves—
something that most Head Start teachers take for granted. During this period, the children had more free-play time, and the schedule relaxed from
one of moving from room to room to occasional moves for music, gym, and
meals. This is the same type of schedule that Judy and Susan described having when the program was located at St. John's.

During the year, the staff pressed Hoover CAC for a more permanent
location. Judy enclosed notes in her packet of monthly paperwork inquiring
about the status of the portable unit. Before Ann met with Starr–Wood River
school officials in January, she asked Judy how things were going. Judy later
recounted, "I told her that things had to work. I want my own space for next
year. I asked her about the portable classroom. She said she would apply for
the money in February. She did not know when she would know about the
funding." During the summer months Judy learned that Hoover CAC had
received funds for a portable classroom unit, but Hoover CAC did not purchase a unit in 1994.

Operating Wood River in Compliance with Head Start Policies

Though the Wood River program was collocated with public school early
childhood programs, the staff was responsible for operating the program in
compliance with Head Start standards. A food temperature problem, which
began in September and continued throughout much of the year, highlighted
how Head Start operated under different policies from those of the other
programs at the Early Learning Center. Gale Jolly, the special education
teacher, asked Gary to bring lunch for her class from Starr to the Early
Learning Center. The special education program served lunch at 11:30 to
accommodate the school's afternoon program schedule, and Head Start
served lunch at 11:45 because Ruth needed time to set the table, butter bread,
and complete other meal preparation tasks. The food caterer packed the food
for both programs in the same container.

When Gale opened the containers to serve her children, the hot foods
quickly cooled. This violated the Hoover CAC food safety policy, which stipulates:

Food prepared or obtained in advance of serving should be held at a temperature of 150 degrees F. or above. . . . If food temperatures are below 150 degrees

F. the caterer should be notified. In most cases the food can be reheated to a temperature of 165 degrees F. and served. . . .

When food is delivered, food containers should remain closed until just prior to serving. (Hoover CAC, n.d.b)

Judy first spoke with Gale and explained that Head Start food policy stipulated that foods be served at specified temperatures and requested that the food containers remain sealed until Ruth opened them to serve lunch. Despite Judy's explanation that Ruth could not prepare the Head Start meal until 11:45, Gale told her that children enrolled in special education had to eat at 11:30 A.M.

Judy then called the Hoover CAC Head Start health component manager, as stipulated in the Hoover CAC food safety policy: "If the food temperatures continue to be a concern the Health Component Manager or Program Dietitian should be notified, and your concern will be addressed to the caterer" (Hoover CAC, n.d.b). Judy talked with Gale again, who was adamant that her children could not wait until Ruth opened the food containers. The special education aide continued to open the food containers at 11:30, 15 minutes before Head Start served lunch.

Judy then called the food vendors and requested that Head Start's foods be packed in separate containers. The food service manager refused, claiming that she did not have separate containers for Head Start's food. The food temperature problem continued from September until March, when Andrea Holland, the Hoover CAC dietitian, came to inspect meal preparation. In the meantime, Ruth reheated hot foods in the microwave and recorded food temperatures, as required by Hoover CAC policies.

When Andrea inspected the food service procedures in March, she asked Ruth if she had checked the temperature on the porcupine meatballs. Porcupine meatballs, a delicacy dating back to the 1960s, are composed of hamburger mixed with rice. Ruth later told me, "I stuck the thermometer in the meatballs, and they weren't up to temperature. We put the meatballs in the microwave for 2 minutes and they still weren't up to temp. So they went back in the microwave for 5 minutes and they still weren't at temperature. Andrea, she wasn't pleased."

Ruth laughed. "I guess what she learned is there's a difference between policy and what goes on here."

Andrea's response to the meatball incident was to call the food service manager and request that Head Start foods be packaged in separate containers. The food service manager, who had ignored Judy's request in September, did comply with Andrea's request, and the following day the foods arrived in separate containers. Though Judy was vested with the power and authority of site manager, she was not successful in rectifying the food container problem.

The food temperature problem created tension between the Head Start program and special education program staffs. Judy both asserted Head Start policy and tried to maintain friendly relationships with Gale. The food temperature problem also signifies the difference between Head Start monitoring and Starr–Wood River school district monitoring. Head Start facilities and meal-serving procedures are systematically monitored by the Hoover CAC Head Start administrative staff. The program dietitian and health component manager each inspected the program twice during the year. Ruth, as required, took weekly food temperatures and submitted this information to Hoover CAC. Gale's program is not subject to meal inspections or weekly food temperatures, but operates under a different set of policies and procedures. This difference was evident in a comment that Gale made to me at the end of the 1993–94 school year: "It seems that Head Start staff spend all their time on paperwork and nutrition, not that those aren't important, but are those the things that are really important? Look at how long it took to work out that thing with the lunches, that was ridiculous."

From Gale's perspective, how Head Start operates is not congruent to the way that her program operates. Yet despite the differences in program policies, Gale, more than other Early Learning Center staff, worked with Judy to develop cooperative activities.

THE PRACTICE OF COOPERATIVE PROGRAMMING

Gale approached Judy at the start of the year and invited Head Start to join her class for music 3 days per week. Judy accepted this offer, and we brought the children next door for music, but we were not involved in curriculum planning for the joint class. I once volunteered to bring my autoharp and play with Gale, but she thought that her guitar might not be in tune with my instrument. I did not press the matter further, assuming that Gale was more comfortable planning and orchestrating the class on her own.

The music time began with a "hello" song and then children selected songs to sing from a song board at the front of the room. The song board had three cardboard strips holding cards with pictures depicting different songs. For instance, the song "Clap, Clap, Clap Your Hands" had a picture of clapping hands. Gale used cards with the children's names written on them to select the child who chose the song. The selected child picked one song card from the board, and Gale asked, "What song is that?" After the child answered, Gale played the tune on her guitar, and the children and teachers sang along. The songs that Gale chose followed seasonal themes: In the fall we sang songs about colored leaves, squirrels, Halloween, and Thanksgiving.

After Thanksgiving came songs about Christmas followed by winter and Valentine songs. Toward March the songs switched to circus and spring themes.

In addition to sharing in music classes, Head Start participated in a schoolwide Halloween sing-along and a visit with police officers. During the police visit, Sarah cried and Ben talked loudly while the policeman spoke. Following this activity, a kindergarten teacher told Judy that she should make her own arrangements for the Head Start children to visit the fire station. Judy and Gale jointly planned a party to celebrate Mickey Mouse's birthday, and Judy arranged for a special cake. Ruth set up a karate demonstration and invited Gale's class to join Head Start. Judy and several Head Start parents attended a discipline workshop offered by Gale and sponsored by the Starr–Wood River community education program. Judy later told me that it was the best workshop she had ever attended on the topic.

At the first parent meeting at the end of September, Carol Blake, the parent educator in the family education program, talked about her program and the services available to children and parents. Following the presentation, one parent signed her child up for a kindergarten preparation class called learning readiness class. The class operated 2 mornings per week from 9 to 11 A.M. in the classroom that Head Start shared with the family education program. In the spring, Carol gave Judy information about the upcoming family education classes, and two additional Head Start parents signed their children up for the learning readiness class.

The other staff at the Early Learning Center invited Head Start staff to join them for birthday celebrations, lunchtime potluck dinners, and staff parties. Judy explained that we were required to eat lunch with the children and could not regularly participate in lunchtime celebrations. We would occasionally take a few minutes and join the other staff, but did not make a regular practice of joining in lunchtime gatherings.

Until 1993 Head Start had operated in isolation from other Wood River early childhood programs. The move to the Early Learning Center prompted Head Start, special education, family education, and kindergarten staff to participate in cooperative activities. Although the activities did not change the basic structure of the programs, they did promote more communication among the staff. One of the outcomes of this communication was the identification and serving of two Head Start children eligible for special education services.

Dually Serving Children

In September Gale conducted preschool screening for all children residing in the Starr–Wood River school district. Through this initial screening and later testing, Allison and Jasmine, two girls enrolled in Head Start, qualified for early childhood special education services. During the assessment process, Gale Jolly and the speech therapist observed Allison and Jasmine in their Head Start activities and assessed them on an individual basis. Allison's and Jasmine's parents gave permission for the school district to provide their children with specialized services.

Following the assessments, the special education staff and Judy met with Allison's and Jasmine's parents to explain the test results. Since the 1970s, federal Head Start policy has mandated that 10% of the children served in Head Start should be those identified with special education needs. Children with special education needs are served in classes with their typically developing peers, and auxiliary services, such as aides and therapy, are provided during regularly scheduled classes. In the 1990s it was common for Head Start and special education programs to dually serve young children with disabilities, and when the special education staff and Judy met with Allison's and Jasmine's mothers, they agreed that the girls remain in Head Start and that the special education staff would provide additional services to them during the Head Start day. In this instance Head Start and the special education program collaborated in providing services to the children dually enrolled in their programs. Judy had frequent and ongoing contact with Gale and other support staff members about Jasmine and Allison. In addition, Judy would ask Gale to observe other children whom she felt might benefit from special education services.

One of the services available to Allison and Jasmine was adaptive physical education. This was the class conducted by Grace during the morning art class. When Judy was informed of this service, she stated, "I don't want these children singled out for services." Grace agreed to conduct a session for the entire Head Start class.

Grace already provided similar services to children in family education classes who did not qualify for special education services but were enrolled in a combined class with the special education program. Special education programs, like Head Start, were under federal and state mandates to collaborate with community-based early childhood programs. More and more services for children identified with special education needs were provided in mainstream settings where all children participated in the activities.

Judy arranged for Allison to move from the second bus route to the first so that she could attend the gym class. Gym was scheduled on Monday, Tuesday, and Thursday from 10:40 to 11 A.M. The children on the first bus route attended the full class and the children on the second bus route attended half of the class. Three days per week for 20 minutes, the Head Start children worked on large- and small-muscle activities such as throwing balls, walking a balance beam, skipping, hopping, and jumping.

Staff were also concerned about Sarah's and Ben's abilities to answer simple questions. For instance, when Judy asked Sarah, "What is your dog's name?" She would sometimes respond, "Blue." Ben did not use first-person pronouns and referred to himself as "he." The special education staff, through informal contacts and daily music classes, had observed both Sarah and Ben and shared the Head Start staff's concerns about their language skills. Sarah's father refused to have the school district assess her for special education services. Sarah's older brother had been identified for special education services, and her father felt that the label had been detrimental. Ben's mother agreed to the assessment but decided that she did not want a special education plan for Ben. Judy then asked Sarah's and Ben's parents for permission for their children to join Allison and Jasmine for speech class. They agreed. Allison, Jasmine, Ben, and Sarah attended a speech class with the speech therapist following lunch on Mondays, Tuesdays, and Thursdays.

During her spring conference with Sarah's father, Judy learned that he did not plan to send her to kindergarten the following fall. He felt that she was too immature to start school because she did not turn 5 until shortly before the school entry deadline. He felt that Sarah needed another year to mature and decided to send her to a home day care program for the upcoming year.

Judy told me that it was too bad that Head Start could not serve Sarah in the upcoming year. Head Start regulations prohibit programs from serving children who are school-age eligible even if the staff or parents recommend that the child delay entry into kindergarten. In the spring when Judy and I had a discussion regarding this policy, she argued that it would be best for Sarah to stay in Head Start for the upcoming year, and I claimed that what Sarah needed was a program that could address her language difficulties, a program such as Gale Jolly's special education program. Judy pointed out correctly that parents decided whether to have their children assessed, and if the children qualified, they were served in a program such as Gale's. If Head Start policy did permit Sarah to enroll as a 5-year-old, she would have been eligible for all the services she was receiving, which did include some speech and language services.

Despite her father's decision that Sarah would not be assessed and "labeled" as a child with a problem, Judy arranged for speech and physical education services for her. These services would probably have been provided to Sarah if she had been assessed and had qualified for special education. If Sarah had returned to Head Start the following year, she would have continued to receive the same services.

At the end of the year, Judy said that one thing she would do differently the following year would be to refer children to Gale earlier in the fall. Judy explained that until this year she had had little contact with Gale and her staff and that it was helpful to have them close by.

Tiny Tales of Success

As noted earlier, Judy honored parents' rights to refuse special education services for Ben and Sarah and at the same time obtained their permission for the children to join Jasmine and Allison for speech class. Though Ben and Sarah were not officially served by the special education staff, they received the same physical education and speech services for which they would have been eligible if they had qualified for special education services.

Judy's insistence that the gym teacher include all the Head Start children in the speech class and her partnership with Gale to provide speech services to Ben and Sarah are examples of how the Wood River staff defined the program's mission and philosophy. At Wood River, all children were to be included in gym class, not only the ones eligible for services. This practice reflected current special education practice, called inclusion, which consists of serving identified children in the company of their peers.

Judy's decisions to provide services to Sarah and Ben and to include all children in the gym class are what I call "tiny tales of success," local solutions to a problem or issue that may or may not transfer to another program. Judy had a working relationship with Gale and developed a way in which to include Sarah and Ben in the needed speech and language class without officially labeling either child with an identified disability. Perhaps in another Head Start program the teacher would not have the necessary relationship with the special education teacher for such an arrangement. But at Wood River this was possible, and Judy, with Gale's willing assistance, arranged for help for both Sarah and Ben.

Difficulties in Expanding Cooperation

Gale invited Judy to attend a regional collaboration workshop sponsored by the state's special education division. The day-long workshop, scheduled for April, was designed for special education programs collaborating with other programs. Ruth attended in Judy's place because Judy was attending the National Head Start Association Conference in Louisville. Following the workshop, Ruth reported, "It was interesting. What they talked about was Head Start and special education doing much more together. [The speaker] described how in some programs the special education and Head Start teachers plan themes together. Within these themes, they decided how to provide specialized services to the children who qualify for them."

Ruth continued, "I am sure that it would take some time to get it started, at the beginning. But it really sounded neat once they got it going."

Judy responded, "As it stands now there are only 2 weeks in the year when we don't have required units." Judy felt that the required curriculum would make if difficult for her to do more joint planning with Gale. Over time, the collaborative activities with Gale's class decreased; by the 3rd year, Head Start no longer joined her class for music.

EXAMINING POLICY IMPLICATIONS

Differing Experiences with Collocation

For the Hoover CAC administrators, the collaboration policy entailed collocating Head Start programs with other early childhood programs. For the Wood River staff, collocation was a series of year-long events that began with the move to the Early Learning Center. One explanation for the difference between the administrative view and the staff experience of the collaboration policy is that the administrators view time differently and operate under distinctly different time frames. Hargreaves (1994) suggests that Edward Hall's model of monochronic and polychronic conceptions of time is useful in explicating the differences between teachers' and administrators' views of time. Administrators who operate according to monochronic time generally concentrate on one thing at a time and view a project as a series of linear progressive stages. In this frame, comments Hargreaves:

> There is little sensitivity to the particularities of context or the needs of the moment within this time-frame. It is the schedule and its successful completion that have priority. Within such work, the completion of tasks, schedules and procedures predominates over the cultivation of relationships with people. (p. 102)

From a monochromic perspective, the collaboration policy was interpreted as collocating Head Start with other early childhood programs. Collocation entailed negotiating a contract with the Starr–Wood River district and moving the materials from St. John's to the Early Learning Center. Head Start shared "time" and "space" with other programs, and the regular activities of the Head Start day were molded to "fit" into the available time and space.

But for the Wood River staff the move was not a one-day event or occasional meeting with school administrators, but a series of events that began in August and continued throughout the school year. Hoover CAC administrators negotiated the rental agreement and periodically conducted on-site evaluations, but for the staff the move was many events happening simultaneously. The staff moved the program; developed and maintained relationships with family education, special education, and kindergarten programs; and figured out how to arrange the schedule around the other programs. The

Wood River staff experienced the move in terms of polychronic time, because they had to "concentrate on doing several things at once, in combination" (Hargreaves, 1994, p. 102). In polychronic time frames, "there is heightened sensitivity to context, to the implications and complications of immediate circumstances and surroundings" (p. 102).

For the Wood River staff, "heightened sensitivity to context" entailed accommodating to the Early Learning Center and pressing for a more permanent location. Staff "made do" in working around the other program's schedules, but the Wood River staff all agreed that the situation was intolerable. During some especially frustrating periods, Judy said that she wanted to quit or that she would refuse to work unless Hoover CAC procured a mobile unit.

I think that administrators held a different view of the situation. They had fleeting glances of the Wood River program when they conducted on-site evaluations, but they did not experience what it was like to operate in the environment day after day. When Ann Norstrom and Martha Calle asked Judy how things were going, she generally stated that we were "making the best of it." That was true. On the other hand, the administrators, lacking an understanding of working under the difficult circumstances at Wood River, needed more direct information on the daily schedule, disruptions, and problems. As Martha Calle said, "Sometimes you have to be obnoxious to get heard." Judy often said that she did not want others to see her as a "nag." Perhaps in this situation more nagging would have been useful.

When staff did voice concerns about room arrangements or meal problems, or ask about the mobile unit, administrative responses were often delayed and sometimes evasive. For instance, in October, 3 months before the actual installation, Martha Calle expressed her surprise that the gym divider was not in place. I assumed that she would investigate the delay and report back to us. Judy voiced her frustration about the divider when she said, "If they [office staff] had to work like this just one day, it would be up real fast." Staff's frustration level about the mobile unit mounted as our queries to administrators about funding and construction dates were left unanswered. After having survived the first year, staff had hoped to move into a mobile unit before the fall. During the summer, staff learned that we would return to the Early Learning Center again and were given no assurances about construction of a mobile unit.

Obstacles to True Collaboration

In the wake of the 1994 Head Start collaboration initiative, Judy described the structural limits of sharing space and mandates imposed by Hoover CAC that make true collaboration difficult. In this case, various layers of Head

Start structure and policy conflict. On the one hand, programs are required to collaborate, and on the other, they are required to work under the same rules and regulations that have in the past served to isolate Head Start from other community programs.

Because the Starr–Wood River school district administered the special education, family education, and kindergarten programs, they operated under a similar districtwide set of policies governing the school schedule, staff qualifications, and operating procedures. Head Start operated under a different set of policies that, at times, were in conflict with districtwide practices. The difference in these procedures is captured in the comment included earlier from Gale Jolly at the end of the 1993–94 year: "It seems that Head Start staff spend all their time on paperwork and nutrition, not that those aren't important, but are those things that are really important? Look at how long it took to work out that thing with the lunches, that was ridiculous." Gale's comment that paperwork and nutrition are not the most important things indicates that her program operates under different rules from those of Head Start.

The Wood River staff found themselves in a triple bind: Head Start's low status provided little access to either rooms or resources; they were required to operate the program in compliance with federal, state, and agency policies; and they needed to maintain an atmosphere of civility with the other Early Learning Center staff. Head Start's secondhand status among the Early Learning Center programs hampered collaboration. Head Start staff operated at a distinct disadvantage to other programs because most of the program's equipment and supplies were in storage, staff had limited access to classroom space, and the daily schedule entailed multiple moves from room to room. If the relationships between Head Start and the other Early Learning Center programs had started out on a more equal basis, then it is likely that the daily operation would have been different. If Head Start, like the other Early Learning Center programs, had regular classroom space and support services, including building maintenance that complied with Head Start and child care licensing policies, then the Wood River staff would be faced with fewer obstacles.

Exploring Collaboration

I agreed with Judy that if Head Start had more permanent space it would be possible for more collaboration to occur between Head Start and the special education program. Head Start might also develop more collaborative arrangements with the family education program. In some Head Start programs, family education staff work with Head Start staff in providing parent education programs for the monthly parent meetings. Family education programs, like Head Start, must provide parent education to preschool parents residing in the community, and certified parent educators are well versed in leading discussion groups, presenting information, providing resources, and responding to parents' concerns.

From my viewpoint, the mandated curriculum topics complicate collaboration but do not make it impossible. The question to ask is, What is to be gained or lost by programs collaborating? At the Early Learning Center, three programs—special education, family education, and Head Start—provide preschool programs for 3- and 4-year-old children. It is possible that if the three staff worked more closely together, they could share resources and expertise. However, differences in staff training and certification may be perceived by some as an obstacle. Gale Jolly questioned me several times about why Head Start does not require the same type of teacher certification as do public school programs. Some staff at the Early Learning Center may think that Head Start teachers are less qualified and consequently less capable of collaborative planning. Music class, the one activity in which Head Start and special education children participated regularly as one group, was planned and conducted by Gale.

If the differences in staff training could be addressed in a manner that acknowledges that all teaching staff have a vested interest in joint planning and collaboration, staff would need ongoing and scheduled time to meet and discuss collaborative opportunities. Planning time would probably require administrative approval and fiscal support. It is to be hoped that such support is forthcoming: As I think back to the first year at the Early Learning Center, I remember that Judy developed some of the most innovative and responsive local policies through working with staff in the other Early Learning Center programs.

Despite the difficult circumstances at the Early Learning Center, staff provided daily programs 4 days per week and, under Judy's direction, articulated program models that characterize quality services to children and families. Judy believed that Head Start children eligible for special education services should remain with their peers and negotiated such an arrangement with the physical education teacher. Judy's relationships with Gale and parents who did not choose special education services for their children enabled two children to receive the speech classes they needed. To me, these "tiny tales of success," these policies from practice, are benchmarks of exemplary practice. They are not found in federal, state, or agency policies and regulations but rather in the relationships that staff develop with one other, children, parents, and other professionals.

The collaboration policy was designed to integrate Head Start services with other community-based early childhood programs, to result in higher quality services to children and families. The practices of collocation and cooperative programming at Wood River resulted in both positive and negative outcomes. On the positive side, the program participated in music class and served children with the special education program. Negative outcomes included restricted access to space and resources, disruptive scheduling, and ongoing problems in complying with Head Start policies.

The daily activities at Wood River included complying with Hoover CAC directives such as the daily classroom checklist and collecting in-kind donations. The following story describes the required local-match policy, referred to by the staff as "in-kind."

9

Establishing Policy Priorities

WHERE'D YOU GET ALL THIS STUFF?

It was the end of April. Ruth took her tax-return money and went with her family on a week's vacation to Florida. So I filled in for her, riding the Head Start bus, buckling the kids in, and washing up the dishes after lunch. I was waiting for Gary to come and pick me up. I waited inside the school, near the gym door. Gary pulled up in the white bus and unloaded the first group of children. Judy, who rode the first route, was holding the laundry basket full of backpacks, handing them out as the children got off the bus. She said, "Take your bag and go right inside."

I held the door open and greeted the children as they came in. "Hi, Adam, good to see you. Hey, pick up your backpack, Sarah, or you'll trip and fall."

And the children followed one another down the hall to hang up their backpacks and coats.

Gary and Judy came in, and we stood in the doorway talking. I looked down at the pile of boxes next to the janitor's closet. "What's this?" I asked.

Judy explained, "Parents brought 'em in for in-kind last night." In-kind refers to the Head Start local-match policy. Judy relies heavily on parent donations to meet her monthly in-kind quota.

Gary stopped talking, and we all looked down at the bags of empty toilet paper rolls, egg cartons, and newspaper. Each fall Judy sent a list of items home to parents listing the value of each item. The donated toilet paper rolls and newspapers were worth 5 cents each. The egg cartons were valued at 15 cents.

"Yeah," Judy started, "They brought in over 200 rolls last night. Must get 'em from somewhere. Maybe work. I think maybe someone works at the nursing home. Someone must be saving 'em." Looking over the pile, I calculated that the value of the stuff was close to $30.

Gary smiled.

I asked, "What ya going to do with 'em?"

Judy replied, "They're going right outside to the trash."

"Well, I could take a few of those rolls for our hamsters," I said. I went and got a paper bag to fill up.

Gary and I got on the bus. He was smiling. He closed the bus door and shook his head.

"This in-kind thing," he began. "I don't know. Over the years they sure bring in a lot of junk. There was this one lady once, I can't remember her name, but every day it seemed when we went to pick up her child—now that was back when the parents still rode the bus; we didn't have the paid rider—well, anyway, every day it seemed she handed me a garbage bag full of things. Most of the time it was milk jugs. I would bring 'em back to the center, and she hadn't washed them out or anything. They stunk of sour milk. Had another teacher then; she would take one look at them and tell me, 'trash,' and I would go and throw them away. But the woman, she kept sending this stuff, so one day I said to her, 'Where'd you get all this stuff?' She told me that her sister worked somewhere, maybe A&W, and she saved it for her and brought it over in the garbage bags to donate to school."

Gary laughed. He continued, "So we ended up throwing away A&W's trash that year. Then there was this other one, she started to save baby-food jars. Not only her, but she got all her friends to do it, too. We had so many baby-food jars you couldn't imagine. We could have outfitted everyone in Wood River with baby-food jars."

Gary continued to drive toward Hudson as we talked. The bus bumped along the rough road, full of potholes. I was sitting in the front seat of the bus, right behind Gary, laughing. I said, "Well, I can see why they want people to be involved in the school and all, but this kind of stuff, I don't know. One day this year Brenda was in, and she said to Judy, 'Did you get those plastic jugs I sent you?'" (Brenda's daughter attended Head Start, and she often volunteered her time at the program.)

"Judy looked at Susan and said, 'Do you remember those plastic jugs?' Susan looked puzzled and shrugged her shoulders.

"Brenda pressed on. 'They were real good ones, the heavy plastic ones. My cousin, she gets 'em when she works at McDonald's.'

"All of a sudden Judy livened up. She said, 'Yeah, I remember those. They came all sticky. What did we end up doing with those, Susan, throw them out?'

"Susan answered, 'Yes, I think that we threw them out.'

"'Oh,' said Brenda, 'Next time I will wash 'em out first.'"

As we rode along and chuckled, I thought about Judy and Susan with the bags of plastic containers, egg cartons, newspapers, and magazines.

LOCAL-MATCH POLICY

Head Start policy stipulates that federal Head Start funds be matched with a 20% local match. Local match includes monetary contributions, materials and supplies, volunteer hours, and donated space. Hoover CAC, like other

Head Start grantees, documents local-match contributions and submits this documentation annually to the regional Head Start fiscal office.

During triennial reviews, federal teams inspect the financial management of each grantee. Under the section titled "Compliance with Non-Federal Share," evaluators determine if "the required non-Federal matching funds were provided" (U.S. DHHS, 1993b, p. 117). In the event that grantees do not meet the 20% local-match stipulation, the federal team deems them out of compliance with federal standards and, in some cases, the grantee can be defunded.

Hoover CAC, like other Head Start grantees, devised a plan to comply with the local-match requirement. Hoover CAC divided the total local match required by the number of center- and home-based programs. On August 2, 1990, the policy council approved the in-kind policy, which stipulates that

> the Parent Involvement Coordinator and teachers will explain and stress the importance of "in-kind" contribution at orientation, home visit, parent meetings or on a one-to-one basis throughout the program year (Hoover CAC, 1992b, p. 50).

The local-match policy states that the parent involvement component manager and center-based teachers are responsible for recording and submitting monthly verification of two types of in-kind: volunteer hours and contributions. Volunteer hours included parent participation in the program as classroom assistants, bus riders, kitchen helpers, field trip supervisors and attendees at center or agency meetings, including the monthly parent meetings. Contributions included food donations, items for parties, Campbell soup labels, mileage to and from the center for parent meetings, and materials and equipment for the classroom. Staff received a list of items and the monetary value for each item, which included soup labels, 5¢; mittens, $2.50; play dough, $2.00; cheese, $1.69; and luncheon meat, $2.49. Contributions also included a homework sheet that parents completed monthly, which documented how much time they spent each day with their child doing learning activities such as reading stories, using the telephone, writing, and playing educational games.

At Wood River, Judy was responsible for meeting with parents and explaining the local-match policy. Nora Jacobs, the parent involvement component manager, sent Judy updated forms and information about local match but did not attend parent meetings, though her responsibilities included that she "provide resource information and assistance to parent groups" (Hoover CAC, 1992b, p. 29).

The Hoover CAC *Parent Handbook,* published each year and distributed to all families participating in Hoover CAC Head Start programs, also highlighted the importance of local-match contributions. Five pages of the 44-page handbook contained information about the importance of volunteering and contributions, suggestions for volunteer functions, and contribution and volunteer forms (Hoover CAC, 1993b). The handbook explains that

> in order to receive these [federal] funds, we are obligated to match our total grants with twenty-five per cent of donations. . . . Each volunteer hour is worth $6.25 to the program. It is the responsibility of all parents to volunteer in some way to help meet this obligation. (p. 9)

The pressure that Judy felt to document her monthly quota resulted from the publication and distribution of policy council minutes to Head Start staff and parents. The minutes listed each program individually, the yearly local-match quota, and the local-match total to date.

Meeting the Local-Match Quota

In order to meet the required monthly match quota, Judy, like other Hoover CAC Head Start site managers, relied on three major types of donations: items from the donation list, homework sheets, and volunteer hours. How Judy and the other staff collected these donations is referred to as the practice of in-kind.

As a newcomer to Wood River Head Start, I thought one of the oddest activities was Judy and Susan's counting up, recording, and discarding parent donations of plastic bottles, empty toilet paper rolls, and glass containers. They sat before school started, counted them out, and marked them down on the in-kind form. This form was sent to the office every month, and Judy was then told how much more she needed to fulfill her yearly quota.

"They keep telling me that I don't have enough," she complained. The local-match annual quota for all center-based Hoover CACs was $13,034.16, or $1,372.02 per month. The yearly quota was equivalent to 261,280 empty toilet paper rolls or 2,174 volunteer hours per year, which equals 272 for each month of the Head Start year. In March Judy still had $5,248 of in-kind to collect. Judy and Susan consistently sent home monthly calendars on which parents could record home learning activities and an in-kind contribution form on which parents could list time spent on home learning activities. Parents received a list of 49 suggested activities that included singing, learning to use a seat belt, and visiting the library and were asked to keep track of the time they spent during these activities. Judy then calculated the total number of homework activity hours and multiplied this figure by $6.25. She added this total to the monthly in-kind total. The Hoover CAC Head Start office replied, "Still not enough."

Until 1990 the program had no trouble meeting its monthly total because parents volunteered to ride the bus every day and serve the meals to the children. Judy multiplied the parent volunteer hours by the going hourly rate and added this to her monthly total. Then Hoover CAC hired site aides such as Ruth to ride the bus and prepare the meals. Most of the Head Start parents were then working or in school and couldn't volunteer on a regular basis. During my first year at Wood River, 15 of the 17 Head Start families were headed by parents who either worked or attended school. Nowadays Judy relies more and more on toilet paper rolls and plastic milk containers to meet her monthly quota.

Interpreting Conflicting Policies

At the first parent meeting in September, Judy talked about parent involvement and invited parents to volunteer. In conversations with parents, Judy encouraged them to stop by the program. However, with the exception of one mother, parents did not volunteer on a regular basis. They did respond to Judy's request to assist on field trips, and we were well staffed for these outings.

During my first year at Wood River, one parent, Brenda, regularly volunteered at the program. Her husband worked three jobs to support his wife and three daughters. Brenda, as well as other program volunteers—including parents who supervised field trips, 2 high school volunteers, and me—signed and dated a form each day we volunteered. Judy and Susan then calculated the value of the monthly volunteer hours.

In addition to volunteering, staff called Brenda and asked her to substitute for them. Despite the short notice, Brenda usually found child care for a younger daughter and came in to sub. After Brenda had subbed for her several times, Ruth learned that unlike other paid staff subs, who included a bus driver, former parent, and myself, Brenda was not reimbursed for her time. Judy explained to Ruth that Brenda was entitled to pay but that the program needed her hours to meet the monthly in-kind total.

In this case, Judy depicts the difficulty that staff face when deciding whether to count a parents' hours in the monthly in-kind total or to offer reimbursement for work. Head Start policy clearly states that "parents are one of the categories of persons who must receive preference for employment as non-professionals" (U.S. DHHS, 1970, p. 8). Judy, like Brenda, began as a parent volunteer and then was hired as a program aide. Forty percent of current Head Start staff started as parent volunteers in their children's classrooms.

From an observer's viewpoint, the policies of local match and of hiring parents may not seem in conflict. However, as Judy interpreted these two policies in a program with diminished parent volunteer hours, increasing the monthly in-kind total was given priority. Judy determined that the need to document in-kind took priority over paying parents when they subbed for staff members. After all, for most of Wood River's 25-year history, parents had volunteered and not been reimbursed for their work. When the daily parent volunteers were replaced with site aides, the number of parent volunteer hours plummeted. Judy was under pressure to document a monthly quota of in-kind. She decided that it was more important for the program to work toward meeting the agency quota than to employ Brenda. The local-match policy was given higher priority than the policy to hire parents.

EXAMINING POLICY IMPLICATIONS

Local match is a hallmark of Head Start that dates back to the inception of the program. In order to insure that local communities are committed to and supportive of Head Start, each grantee must document the required 20% match. From a top-down vantage point, the policy appears reasonable. When I examined it from a bottom-up perspective, however, the practice of in-kind is radically different from the federal intent. I attribute this difference to both global and local influences, which include increasing fiscal support for Head Start, Hoover CAC's written policies concerning local match, changes in family demographics, and Wood River staff's interpretations of local-match policies.

Increases in Local-Match Quotas

In my conversations with Head Start directors located in the Midwest, many shared how difficult it has become to procure local-match contributions. In one meeting, Head Start directors asked that funds provided through state allocations be considered part of their federal-match contribution. The federal response at that time was that state dollars could not be used for this purpose. Other directors have solicited large donations such as land and buildings from community groups to meet both their program's facility needs and their local-match quota.

As pointed out, Hoover CAC, like many grantees, had relied on parents to provide daily support for bus riding and meal preparation. These parent volunteers had assured that local programs met or exceeded local-match contributions. As parents entered the labor force in greater numbers, the available pool of volunteers dwindled, resulting in the formulation of a new staff position, that of site aide.

The resulting decrease in volunteer hours was exacerbated because the

Head Start budget doubled between 1990 and 1997, and Head Start grantees like Hoover CAC had to document local-match quotas equivalent to the federal allocations. Grantees were faced with larger local-match quotas with fewer volunteer hours to count toward the yearly total.

Emphasis in Written Policies

Hoover CAC's policies identified that the parent involvement component manager and classroom teachers are responsible for soliciting and documenting volunteer hours and donated goods. The parent involvement component manager monitored in-kind donations from local programs and sent staff forms and information sheets about in-kind, which staff copied and sent to parents. However, the component manager did not meet and talk with parents about in-kind during the 1993–94 school year. The Wood River staff had the responsibility for talking with parents and explaining the local-match policy.

The Hoover CAC parent handbook section on in-kind volunteers begins by stating that "volunteering is essential to the Head Start program. The success and continuation of the program depends upon active participation of parents and others in the community" (Hoover CAC, 1992b, p. 9). The handbook then explains the contributions of parent volunteers in the program: volunteer hours count towards the in-kind quota and volunteers bring skills and knowledge to the program. It is significant that the in-kind value of the volunteer hours is described first, before the discussion about parent contributions to classroom functioning. The textual arrangement of these dual aims are indicative of how important local match is to grantees.

Problems with Parent Volunteering

Parent volunteering at Wood River was minimal. The change in family demographics and, as a result, the addition of site aides are major factors. Others included the difficulty of relying on parent volunteers for regular assistance and staff perceptions of parent availability resulting in diminished efforts to solicit volunteer hours.

In addition to me, two high school students who were enrolled in a community service course volunteered on a fairly regular basis. They arrived prior to lunchtime and helped Ruth with meal preparations. We grew to rely on their help, and when they did not show up, it was more difficult for Ruth to prepare lunch. What I learned from the students' erratic attendance is that the program relied on their help and that on the days when they did not come, the program suffered. In a similar way, Gary described in Chapter 7 the difficulties of relying on parent volunteers to ride the bus and assist with meal preparation. The system worked well as long as parents were reliable but fell apart when Gary arrived to pick up a parent volunteer and found no one at home.

In hiring site aides, Hoover CAC alleviated many of the problems of relying on volunteers to fill the necessary positions of bus rider and meal-service worker and simultaneously responded to the growing number of parents working or attending school. An unintended consequence of hiring site aides is that programs altered their perceptions of parents' volunteering in the classrooms. Staff no longer relied on parents to provide essential services to the program and had to redefine parents' volunteering roles within the new staffing pattern.

Local Attitudes and Efforts

Staff expectations affected how rigorous they were in their efforts to elicit parent volunteer hours. Because staff believed that parents were less available, they did not pursue a rigorous plan to solicit volunteer hours. At Wood River during the 1993–94 year, Judy invited parents to volunteer during the first parent meeting in September. In her conversations with parents, she encouraged them to stop in and visit. When asked, parents did volunteer to supervise children on field trips.

I would characterize Judy's approach as sincere but low profile because she did not make repeated appeals for parent volunteers at parent meetings or in newsletters. For example, Judy did not hand around a monthly calendar at parent meetings and ask parents to volunteer for one day in the upcoming month. This practice was common in some other Hoover CAC centers.

With the decrease in parent volunteer hours, Judy relied heavily on donations and homework sheets to fulfill her monthly in-kind quota. Staff solicited needed items from the contribution list. At staff request, parents sent treats for holiday parties, baby clothes for the dolls, an artificial Christmas tree, and baby-food jars for making Christmas decorations. Parents responded to all staff requests and provided needed resources for the program. Staff threw away most of the unsolicited items, which included egg cartons, toilet paper rolls, bleach bottles, milk cartons, margarine containers, newspapers, and magazines. As I learned from Gary, though the program had not always been as dependent on unsolicited items for in-kind, there was a long history of parents' sending junk to school that staff then threw away.

Each month, as noted earlier, parents received a calendar on which to record their daily activities and an in-kind contribution sheet on which they recorded the total time spent on homework activities and any items donated to the program. When talking with parents or in the monthly newsletter, Judy would remind parents to submit their monthly forms. Many parents did keep track of homework activities and sent in their forms each month. One grand-parent indicated that she had questions about the validity of homework activities. On her second home visit at the end of the year, Judy visited Steven's grandmother, Mrs. Howard, and asked her if she had any in-kind sheets to turn in. Mrs. Howard responded that she did not think parents "should write down things they should be doing anyway." Judy explained why the program needed the hours, but Mrs. Howard took the view that "normal" parent-child activities should not be counted for Head Start volunteer hours.

Pressure to Document

Parents recording homework activities, sending in unsolicited donations, and staff recording and discarding the donations, are examples of procedural displays. The staff established patterns of soliciting homework activity hours and donations not for their local utility but because Hoover CAC required and monitored these activities through reviewing paperwork. At first glance such practices as collecting and discarding in-kind donations seem contrary to the best interests of the staff, children, and families. In-kind donations should be items that the program can use, and parents should engage their children in homework activities because of their interest in the child's development. In these instances, practices are not developed to meet the needs of children and families but to fulfill the requirements outlined in Hoover CAC policies and procedures.

It was the intention neither of Hoover CAC nor of federal policies that parents send in contributions for Head Start staff to discard. Hoover CAC, in developing in-kind policies that included volunteering and contributions, was responding to federal pressure to document a substantial increase in local match that was monitored through annual paperwork and during triennial evaluations of program operations. Both at the agency and local level, the goal was to document the required 20% match. As Ann Norstrom told me several times, "In Head Start, if it is not written down, it does not exist."

The pressure to document in-kind as well as Hoover CAC history influenced Judy's decision to count as volunteer hours those that Brenda worked as a staff substitute. The pre-1990 monetary value of parent volunteer activity has already been noted. In the short run, Brenda helped Wood River to operate smoothly when regular staff were absent. In the long run, Head Start may miss the opportunity to train and employ parents such as Brenda. Head Start has a long history of providing services to children and families. Adult-directed services include literacy classes, training, and mentoring. This two-generational approach "helps low-income parents achieve and maintain self-sufficiency and greater degree of involvement in the education of their children" (U.S. DHHS, 1993a, p. 22).

There was no training plan at Wood River to support the entry of volunteers such as Brenda into paid employment. Other Head Start programs have devised volunteer training programs that prepare parents for employment in nonprofessional staff positions such as site aide and classroom aide. In such programs, parents are expected to volunteer and attend training sessions and gradually move into paid positions.

Brenda, if given the option of a training program leading to paid employment, may have chosen instead to volunteer her time. Brenda was not offered the choice, due in part to the pressure felt by local and agency staff to document in-kind donations. Judy, influenced by Wood River's 25-year history of parent volunteerism, applied Brenda's hours toward the monthly in-kind total.

In other cases, Judy decided that her relationship with the families and children would shape how she interpreted and implemented policies. The following story illustrates how Judy and the staff interpreted child-abuse-reporting policies in relation to Jasmine, a young victim. The story was written by Ruth Donalds shortly after we learned that Jasmine had been sexually assaulted.

10

Understanding Policies Through Relationships

PAINTING RAINBOWS ON PIGS
By Ruth Donalds

That sunny fall day when I first saw Jasmine, she seemed so tiny and frail as she bounded down her stairs toward our bus, straight brown hair flying behind her. She crawled up the bus steps and plopped down in the seat with me.

Gary, the bus driver, and I made our introductions.

I could feel her steel-blue eyes checking me over from head to toe. After a few minutes of this I must have met her approval because a tiny animated voice started to flow from a mouth full of silver-capped teeth.

As the days turned into weeks and Jasmine became comfortable with Gary, myself, and the rest of the children on the bus, she started telling us stories about herself and "her pigs." Once she'd start one of her tales her eyes would light up, and there would be no stopping her until the story was told. One of the stories was about giving her pigs a luxurious bubble bath, then drying them with a hair dryer and combing their hair out. When they were completely done, they'd all lie down and fall asleep.

After each "pig story" I'd question Jasmine as to what kind of pigs they were. "Are they guinea pigs, Jasmine?" I'd ask. She never would answer.

Fall turned into winter and day in, day out, 4 days a week Jasmine would entertain every bright-eyed child, along with Gary and myself, for the first 5 minutes of our bus ride with these elaborate stories. Toward the end she'd throw in, "my neighbor friend, Howard."

Curiosity finally got the best of me one day when Jasmine's mother brought her out to the bus. I asked her if they had any guinea pigs. Jasmine's mother's mouth slowly turned up at the corners, and she replied, "No, but the neighbors raise pot-bellied pigs." (Pot-bellied pigs are a smaller variety of the species that are often raised as household pets.) So those are the pigs in the stories, I thought to myself.

Before long the holidays were put to rest and winter's harshness had started to settle in. The pig stories weren't told much anymore. Only once a week after the children on the bus begged would Jasmine tell them one. The last one I remember hearing was about Jasmine painting rainbows on her pigs.

I'd never known a child like Jasmine before. She could captivate a busload of 4-year-olds with her stories and then get them really going for the entire hour. Then after the children had all been dropped off, she'd become silent and lay her small head on my lap. For that 5-minute trip to her house she'd become so peaceful, almost angelic.

I'd cherish those 5 minutes. Looking down on her, I would wonder how this tiny person could try my patience to the limit, and when I'd almost given up, take a 180-degree turn into a heap of brown hair on my lap.

The teachers and I thought her mother could be an alcoholic, because Judy and Susan noticed open beer cans during a midday home visit. Jasmine, her sister, and her mother lived with "the landlord," Bob Chester. He was a stocky, grumpy man probably twice Jasmine's mother's age, a very domineering type. I'd often wondered what life was really like at home for Jasmine.

One day Susan asked me if I saw the funny way Jasmine had looked, staring at her that day. I hadn't noticed.

Then it happened. On the bus ride home a few days later I looked over at Jasmine, and she was staring at me, but yet through me, with those steel-blue eyes. She almost looked at me as if I was some type of alien from another planet. A chill ran through me. But yet the corner of her mouth was slightly turned up as if in curiosity. At that moment I couldn't find the usual gleam in her eyes; they almost appeared muddy. It was a look I'll never forget, the kind that touches your soul. I tried to imagine what could be running through her mind.

A few weeks later Jasmine, as usual, was the last child on the bus. I had just told her a story about my 7-year-old daughter, Julia. After I was done she looked up at me and asked if she could come over and play with my daughter sometimes. I was caught off guard and told her, "I'll see."

It was another cold, gray, blustery morning as I stood at my window waiting for Gary's honk. I glanced over at the day's paper, and my eyes caught a headline about a Starr man molesting four young girls. The sound of Gary's honk broke my concentration. I grabbed my coat and purse and ran out to greet him.

After I took my usual seat, Gary asked me if I'd read the day's paper.

"No, not really," I said.

He then told me about a "Howard" who had molested four young girls. We hoped that our Jasmine was not one of them. Oh, please, don't let Jasmine be one of them.

I found out the next day that Jasmine hadn't been that fortunate; she was one of the four.

After finding out I went home and went through the motions of preparing dinner. As I was washing the dishes, I looked up through the window out into the cold blackness of the winter night and began to wonder if Jasmine was home in the warmth of her mother's arms. Or if she was in a dark scary room alone while her mother was off somewhere trying to drown her sorrows. My eyes filled with tears, but I couldn't let the dam break until I had safely tucked our children into bed. It would be too hard to try to explain my grief to them.

As I tucked Julia in and kissed her good night a warm tear splattered on her golden hair, only to go unnoticed by her. As I looked at her lying there, so warm, happy, and peaceful, I thought how blessed we are. I never want to leave her or her brother's side for fear of all the Howards in the world.

I walked out of her room and the dam broke. I felt like I'd cry for hours for all of the Jasmines in the world. I wished I could look down and see her small head again on my lap. "Yes, Jasmine, you can come over here and play forever." Here I'd hope she could feel secure and sheltered from anything or anyone that could harm her. All she wants is what is alien to her, a normal family. After the tears finally stopped I feel asleep.

I awoke in the morning with the dark thought of how much permanent damage would be done to this waif of a child. We'll never really know.

As I dug through my jewelry box, I ran across my "Guardian Angel" pin. My grandmother had given it to me a few years ago when we moved. The thought crept into my mind to take it with me today and pin it onto Jasmine's coat. Maybe it would give me just a shred of peace to know she was wearing it, even though it was just a piece of molded metal. Then reality took over. NO! I can't give this or anything to Jasmine. I was told that that's how her friendship with Howard had developed. The giving of small gifts. I didn't want Jasmine to relive this nightmare and wonder if something terrible would happen to her again. No, the only thing that I can give Jasmine was my lap, for 5 minutes, 4 days a week. There she can rest her small head and maybe, just maybe, feel trust, security, peacefulness, and love.

As I watch her lie there, I pray that again someday she'll look up, her eyes illuminated, and open her tiny mouth full of silver-capped teeth and that that animated voice will spill out a wonderful story about painting rainbows on pigs.

We were all stunned to learn that Jasmine had been sexually abused by Howard. Ruth, who had developed a close relationship with her, wrote this story a month after we first learned about what had happened to Jasmine. As staff grappled with how to best meet Jasmine's needs, we worked closely with Bev Beam, Jasmine's mother, and the special education staff, who provided daily services to her.

CHILD ABUSE REPORTING POLICIES

On Wednesday, February 2, an article in the local paper described an older man who was accused of sexually abusing four girls. The next day Ruth and Gary reported that Jasmine was apparently one of this man's victims. Susan, subbing for a vacationing Judy, called Amanda Red, the family advocate for the Wood River Head Start program, to report that Jasmine had been sexually abused. Both state statutes and Hoover CAC policies require that Head Start teachers report cases of child abuse and neglect. Hoover CAC requires all Head Start staff to attend annual training on child abuse and neglect. The Hoover CAC Head Start policy and procedures manual includes a 12-page description of child abuse and neglect and an abuse/neglect reporting form. The manual outlines an eight-step approach for staff to follow if they suspect that a child is a victim of abuse or neglect. The first six steps require that the staff contact the local social services agency and make an official report. The last two steps are as follows:

7. Notify supervisor or Head Start Social Service Coordinator or Director by telephone immediately following report.
8. Complete Abuse/Neglect Reporting Form. Mail to agency. (Hoover CAC, n.d.a)

Implementing the Policy

Susan complied with the reporting policy when she called Amanda Red and reported that Jasmine had been sexually abused. However, later, when she learned that a neighbor had told Ruth about Jasmine, she called Amanda back. The hearsay news from Jasmine's neighbor was problematic. Amanda, intending to call Bev and set up a home visit to discuss Jasmine and offer resources, then redefined the visit in terms of updating information on forms. During the visit, Bev told Amanda that Jasmine had been sexually abused.

Maintaining Family Confidentiality

Bev, we later learned, had already talked with Judy and told her what had happened to Jasmine. The following week, Judy returned from vacation and said that Bev had told her about Jasmine but asked that she not mention it until the incident was reported in the paper. Judy commented to Susan and me, "I really should have told you about it." Judy's decision to maintain a parent's confidentiality could be interpreted as a breach of the official abuse-reporting policy or as an example of a staff member supporting a parent's request. In this instance, Judy knew that Bev and Bev's boyfriend and land-lord, Bob Chester, had filed charges against Howard. The formal-charge process includes a comprehensive child abuse investigation by the Wood River County social services department. This process is the same as outlined in the first six steps of the Hoover CAC Head Start child abuse reporting procedures. Judy failed to follow steps requiring her to contact Hoover CAC and to follow up this contact with a completed reporting form. In maintaining the family's confidentiality, Judy set the stage for working with Bev and letting her know that the staff would listen and respond to her requests.

DEFINING JASMINE AS AN ABUSE VICTIM

On February 16, Judy, Susan, Ruth, and I discussed our observations of Jasmine. I mentioned that she hid under the table during art. Susan told Judy that Jasmine hid in the bathroom. I said, "It's too bad that we couldn't get some more information about what to do. I just don't know how to handle things."

Judy replied, "You wonder if you should be saying something to her or just let it pass. It might make it worse."

Later in the day Judy said, "I wonder if we couldn't get a meeting with Amanda and Bev and the three of us to talk about Jasmine and what we could do."

Judy then called Bev and Amanda and set up the meeting for Monday, February 28. Judy told Martha Calle, the Wood River county coordinator, about the meeting, and Martha suggested that Judy consult with Jasmine's therapist and that Head Start would be willing to pay a consultation fee.

Though the Wood River staff were certain that Jasmine's behavioral changes were the result of her sexual abuse trauma, Martha Calle asked if Jasmine's daily medication for attention deficit disorder was responsible for the changes. Judy explained, "This behavior is all new in the last 2 to 3 weeks, and she has been on medication since the beginning of the year." We then listed our observations of the changes in Jasmine's behavior.

I was surprised that Martha questioned our analysis of Jasmine's behavior. In reviewing a handout distributed by Hoover CAC to Head Start staff, withdrawn and fearful behaviors, which Jasmine exhibited, are listed as indicators of sexual abuse trauma. For those of us who worked with her, these changes were self-evident. But Martha had not witnessed them.

MEETING WITH JASMINE'S MOTHER

Bev, Bob Chester, Amanda, Martha, Judy, Susan, and I met on February 28 to discuss Jasmine's school behavior. Bev explained that she had spoken with Jasmine's therapist:

What Jasmine is doing is right in line with what should be going on. School used to be her safety net, and then when this all came out, school isn't safe anymore. The last time she went home, someone hurt her. Howard. This comes out, the places used to be safe like school, she doesn't think of them like that anymore. The therapist says we have to find something or somebody that will make her think school is a safe place to be.

Bob spoke next:

I had all my guns in the shop that week. Otherwise I would have taken them an' hurt him. Lots of dads in the neighborhood right now like to hurt him. Say that we can't do that. End up in jail.

Bev added:

Given his age, they don't think he'll serve any time. Probably probation. Might send him to someplace for a few months. Could move right back to where he lives now. That's th' hard thing right now. He's out there and when the bus comes, Jasmine won't go outside until the bus is in the driveway. Giving us a hard time getting ready for school. She says that she doesn't want to go. She is fine once the bus is in the driveway, but you know, Ruth, our driveway runs right into Howard's. That is what is hard about it right now. He's still out there and when the bus comes, Jasmine won't go outside until the bus is in the driveway.

Martha suggested, "Maybe Gary could drive up in the yard further. That would help?"

Bob replied, "Yeah, and you tell him that I didn't say anything 'bout him being on my lawn." Apparently Bob had spoken several times to Gary about keeping off the lawn.

Judy asked, "So you aren't noticing anything at home?"

Bev answered, "At night, she won't go to sleep unless there is a light on. Whatever he did to her, did it in the dark. They're hoping that in 6 months or so she'll tell us what he did. Then they can use that an' charge him with those counts too."

Judy asked what the Wood River staff could do to make Jasmine feel safe. Bev said that the therapist had told her that it was important for Jasmine to develop a relationship with at least one staff member to whom she could turn if she felt upset. Bev suggested that the therapist might help staff with more ideas. Bev signed the forms authorizing the therapist to release Jasmine's records to Head Start. Martha repeated her suggestion that Hoover CAC would be willing to pay for a consultation with the therapist so that staff would get some help in understanding Jasmine and set up a plan to meet her needs. Jasmine's psychological records never did reach Wood River. It is possible that they were sent to Hoover CAC and were not forwarded to Judy.

In meeting with Bev and Bob, we got a better understanding of how Jasmine was affected by the abuse and how we might support her. We could understand their frustration that Howard was still living next door and Bob's desire to physically harm him. We worried what would happen to Jasmine and her sister, another victim, if Howard remained in the neighborhood.

HELPING JASMINE'S HEALING PROCESS

For the next 2 months the staff provided additional support for Jasmine. She frequently asked one of us to hold and hug her. On one occasion, right before going home, she asked me to hold her, and I told her to first put on her coat. Four-year-old June then asked visiting Martha to hold her. Jasmine put on her coat and then asked to be held. I picked her up and held her. Later Martha told me she had talked with the staff and explained that for safety reasons Hoover CAC did not recommend that staff pick up the children. It was preferable to sit and hold them instead.

Though I understood the rationale for this policy, I, like the other staff, often disregarded it when Jasmine asked to be held. Sometimes we did sit and hold her, but other times, especially when in the hall, we picked her up. The Wood River staff had decided that holding Jasmine was appropriate even if it sometimes meant that we picked her up.

Ruth reported that Bev did not accompany Jasmine down to the bus but stayed at the house. Bev later told us that Jasmine would not let her bring her to the bus but insisted on going alone. Gary drove into the yard to block Jasmine's view of Howard's yard. Ruth then got off the bus and helped Jasmine to get on. Gary commented, "I knew that this would happen. A couple of the kids asked why Ruth got out to help Jasmine, and I told them that Ruth was afraid that Jasmine would fall. But you can't be doing that with her and not have the others ask for the same treatment. That's not fair."

Gary questioned how Jasmine was being treated because it affected what the other children then asked for. Ruth did not treat Jasmine in the same way as she did the other children, but I think she treated her and the other children fairly. In working with young children, teachers are told to treat children fairly. But fairly does not mean equally (Katz & McClellan, 1991). Ruth, as did Judy, Susan, and I, accommodated Jasmine's need for holding and extra support.

Ruth asked Judy about Jasmine's request to visit Ruth at home. Judy advised Ruth not to invite her for a visit, cautioning that Bev might take advantage of her hospitality. In this case Judy differentiated between staff's responsibilities to accommodate Jasmine's special needs and the limits of our involvement with her family.

Jasmine refused to go to speech class, so the speech therapist brought a few of Jasmine's favorite toys from the speech room to the Head Start class. On some days Jasmine refused to go to Gale Jolly's room for music, and a staff member would stay with her in our room. When she did join Gale's class for music, Jasmine would sit in a staff's lap and listen. Judy kept Gale and the speech therapist informed of any new developments concerning Jasmine and in this way enlisted their help in supporting her through this difficult time.

Jasmine's behavior continued to trouble us. She pinched, hit, and shoved other children. She yelled if a child "looked at" her. On the bus Jasmine screamed, persisting despite Ruth's attempts to quiet her down. When Ruth and Gary asked for suggestions to quiet her down, Judy suggested that they explain the problem to Bev. If the screaming continued, Bev would then have to transport Jasmine to and from school. At the end of April when I subbed for Ruth, Jasmine was loud and uncooperative on the bus. Sitting by her did not calm her and neither did isolating her from the rest of the group. When I asked Gary for suggestions, he shook his head and said that this was what he and Ruth were struggling with. I mentioned to Bev when we dropped Jasmine off that we were having difficulty with her on the bus. Despite these outbursts, however, Ruth and Gary continued to transport Jasmine to and from school.

By the end of the school year Jasmine had returned to the speech therapist for daily class with her three classmates and had begun to sing in music class again. In the last weeks of school Jasmine returned to the housekeeping area and played there for the first time in 3 months. We discussed these changes, and in April Susan noted that for the first time in months Jasmine was playing again. She hid under tables less and was more apt to join the children in running around the gym after lunch. We took note of instances when Jasmine laughed, "acted wild," and told stories. We saw these as signs that she was returning to her "old" behavior patterns. As Jasmine's behavior shifted, we expected her to comply with classroom rules. If she received a warning to be quiet during circle time and continued to talk, Judy or Susan would tell her to sit on a chair near the group until she could settle down. Though we seldom welcomed wild behavior, we saw this as a positive sign that Jasmine was beginning the healing process.

However, we learned that Jasmine's home behavior was still disturbed. In early May, Gary drove Jasmine home, but Bev was not there, so he brought her back to Wood River. By the time Gary and Jasmine arrived back at Head Start, Bev, frantically trying to locate Jasmine, had called Judy. Judy assured Bev that Jasmine was fine and said that Susan and she would give her a ride home. When they arrived at her house, Jasmine brought Susan and Judy out to see her bunny. Bev explained that Jasmine had swung the rabbit over her head and broken his legs. Bev said that Jasmine was kicking and hurting the dog.

In September 1994, Howard was found guilty of sexual assault. He was sentenced to a treatment program and was required to move to a new location. Prior to his conviction, he had been incarcerated for verbally threatening several of the girls he had assaulted.

EXAMINING POLICY IMPLICATIONS

Family Confidentiality Versus Official Reporting Policy

In "Painting Rainbows on Pigs" Ruth Donalds describes how she developed a special fondness for Jasmine during the daily bus ride to and from Head Start. Ruth's story draws attention to the importance of personal values in the response to Jasmine's situation.

Judy had established a relationship with Bev, Jasmine's mother, during the fall when Jasmine was assessed for special education services. Bev confided in Judy that Jasmine had been assaulted and asked that Judy maintain the family's confidentiality. Judy, in honoring this request, adhered to the Hoover CAC confidentiality policy, which states that confidentiality "includes not only the correct method for maintaining files and disseminating and sharing of information . . . it is an attitude of respect for the value of each parent and child in our program" (Hoover CAC, 1993a, p. 1).

The problem that resulted from Judy's maintaining Bev's confidentiality occurred because Judy was on vacation when we heard that Jasmine had been sexually assaulted. This situation, more than others that occurred during Judy's absence, highlights the crucial nature of her position at the program.

Susan, unaware of Judy's communications with Bev, filed a report with Hoover CAC that complied with stated child abuse and neglect reporting procedures. Head Start staff, like teachers and child care workers, are mandated, under penalty of law, to report any cases of suspected child abuse or neglect to the local law enforcement or child protection agency. From a top-down vantage point, the mandated reporting policy is essential to providing protection to children. The staff's initial reports to Hoover CAC and the law enforcement agency are followed by a formal inquiry conducted by county

child protection workers, to determine if the charges warrant a full investigation. In Jasmine's case the investigative process resulted in formal charges
being filed against Howard.

Lack of Professional Training and Support

The Wood River staff recognized the seriousness of Jasmine's situation, but
lacked the knowledge and skills to support her. Head Start staff, like other
teaching staff, receive training about mandated reporting, but not on working
with victims of abuse. In meeting with Bev and Bob, we got a better understanding of how Jasmine was affected by the abuse and how we might support her.

Under Judy's leadership, we devised local policies from practice, which
included honoring Jasmine's request to stay in the classroom during music
and speech therapy sessions. Contrary to the Hoover CAC recommendation
that I learned about from Martha, we picked Jasmine up and held her. In
view of Jasmine's situation, Martha's comment seemed out of context. My
reasoning for picking her up was that that a victim of sexual abuse had special needs that required special accommodation. In a similar manner, despite
Gary's concern that children would think it unfair, Ruth decided to accompany Jasmine on the bus each morning.

Although Bev had signed a permission form to release copies of Jasmine's therapy records to the program, the records never reached Wood
River. It is hard to know if they would have contained information helpful
to the staff. However, consulting with the therapist, as Martha suggested,
might have aided staff in their efforts to support Jasmine. The therapist might
have shared her perceptions of Jasmine's condition and helped staff devise
strategies to cope with Jasmine's defiant and aggressive behavior at the center
and on the bus. The consultation may have assisted staff in their efforts to
help Jasmine and in future efforts to assist other children and families en-
countering sexual abuse trauma.

Policies from Practice

In a view of child abuse from a bottom-up perspective, the official confidentiality and child abuse reporting policies appear to be interwoven with the
local policies that staff devised in working with Jasmine and her family. Staff
worked at the crossroads of families' needs and the mandates of rules and
procedures. Susan complied with the official child abuse reporting policy by
filing the required report. However, the official reporting policy had little
impact on our daily interactions with Jasmine. In our daily work with her,
we devised policies from practice, which included holding her, accompanying

her on the bus, adjusting the daily schedule to support her needs, and maintaining communication with her mother. We developed these local policies
out of our relationships with Jasmine and Bev and our understanding of what
would work best for the family and program staff.

Ruth's story about Jasmine highlights how staff interpreted official policies in the context of the needs of the children and families. In other cases,
such as paying parents for volunteer hours, staff interpreted official policies in
terms of complying with monthly in-kind quotas. In the concluding chapter I
return to the four questions posed in Chapter 1 to discuss how policy is defined, how staff interpret and negotiate official policies, negotiate local needs,
and develop policies in response to local needs. I also discuss the implications
of this study for Head Start reform efforts.

11

Conclusion

Another year at Wood River Head Start. Much is the same, and some has changed. The Wood River Head Start staff is all back this year. Judy was right, we are in the Early Learning Center again. Hoover CAC did receive funding during the summer to purchase a mobile classroom unit. In October Judy met with the Head Start director and an architect to draw up plans for the unit. It is self-contained and will have a bathroom, kitchen, and classroom. At the December 1994 meeting, the Wood River school board approved the construction of the portable unit in the parking lot of the Early Learning Center. It is hoped that construction will begin in the spring of 1995.

In October Martha and I walked by the Wood River, and Steven came out to talk with me. He is a kindergartner at St. John's this year and told me, "I like school a lot." This year we have 14 new children and three children returning from last year. Mark's mother never returned his medical examination form, so he could not enroll in Head Start this fall.

We see Jasmine almost every day. She, Ben, and Allison are now in half-day kindergarten and in Gale Jolly's room for the other half of the day. Judy and I saw her mother, Bev, last week and spent some time in small talk with her. An article in a local newspaper quoted several girls who were victim to Howard's attacks. One said, "I have a hard time sleeping at night. I have bad dreams and I'm very scared of him."

This year we tell each other some of the stories of last year. We worry about Jasmine. Now the stories of last year play against the present. These stories are told and retold, becoming smoother with each telling. When I asked Judy about Mark she said, "That was so long ago, I can hardly remember it." We forget about the rough edges of when we first told the stories to one other. We forget how it was to sit with Mark each day when the bite-of-protein policy first started.

Perhaps this spring workers will start construction on the mobile unit. For now we are in the gym doing art, sharing the room with the family education program. For now it is winter. For now we sit and share the stories of today and yesterday.

I realize that it is through these everyday conversations and work that the Wood River staff taught me how to interpret policies: Gary remembered how it was to operate without transportation policies; Ruth knew the difference between official policies and the realities of the Early Learning Center kitchen; Susan described the importance of complying with regulations; and Judy questioned the prescriptive nature of many Head Start policies. During this year and last I have wondered: How is policy made and defined? Who does the defining? For me, these questions are answered in the daily interchanges or stories that we at Wood River tell each other.

Local events, such as eating with Mark, counting and recording in-kind donations, and finding out that Howard sexually abused Jasmine, are central to my understanding of how the Wood River staff interpret, implement, and create policies. In Chapter 1, I posed four questions for this study: How is policy defined in a local Head Start program? How do staff interpret and negotiate official public policies such as the federal Head Start performance standards, licensing regulations for child care centers, and Hoover CAC agency and Head Start policies? How do local staff negotiate federal and agency policy and local needs? How do staff develop local policies to respond to the ongoing needs and specific problems in the daily operation of the program? In the following sections, I first respond to each of these questions, and then discuss the implications of this study for Head Start reform efforts. I end the chapter with an Epilogue describing recent developments at Wood River.

HOW IS POLICY DEFINED IN A LOCAL PROGRAM?

The Wood River staff "live out" the daily implementation of a Head Start program as defined by official policy. Official policies define a program and the program's characteristics: determining the program clientele, staffing pattern, and program components. Official Head Start policies that define program operations at local programs are developed by a federal, state, and administrating agency: the U.S. Department of Health and Human Services, the state Department of Human Services, and the grantee agency. The federal policies outline a course of action for Head Start programs, the state policies outline a course of action for programs licensed as child care facilities, and the agency policies outline a course of action for agency staff employed in Head Start positions. The courses of action are specific enough to give some direction to local staff but broad enough to be subject to multiple local interpretations.

How a policy is delineated depends upon the vantage point that is taken in defining that particular policy. A vantage point, or viewing position, draws attention to certain policy processes. Top-down vantage-point analysis refers to how federal, state, agency, and local staff interpret and implement official policies. Bottom-up vantage-point analysis focuses on how local Head Start staff develop and implement local policies, called policies from practice, in response to local needs and emergency situations. The same policy is defined differently depending upon whether one examines it from a top-down or bottom-up vantage point. For example, from a top-down vantage point, the child abuse and reporting policies described in the story about Jasmine are defined as complying with state and agency reporting procedures. From a bottom-up perspective, the policy is defined by the practices that staff developed to support Jasmine and her family in their healing process.

Policy is defined by those members of federal, state, agency, and community program organizations vested with power and authority. It was the federal review team that determined that St. John's was out of compliance with Head Start standards and required that that the program be relocated. The state child care licensing agent determined that the classroom at the Early Learning Center was too small to accommodate 18 children and issued a license stipulating that the program could serve no more than 17 children. Hoover CAC administrators, through on-site evaluations and review of paperwork, determined whether the Wood River program operated in compliance with agency policies. At the local level, Judy, vested with the power and authority of the site-based manager, had the most influence in defining policy.

Wood River staff refer to all policies as Hoover CAC policies because Hoover CAC distributes a policy manual containing federal, state, and agency policies. At this level Hoover CAC administrators define official operating policies reflective of their interpretation of federal, state, or agency policies. Staff learn about these policies by attending agency Head Start meetings, asking Hoover CAC staff for clarification on policy-related questions, talking among themselves, and discussing policies at monthly team meetings.

HOW DO STAFF INTERPRET AND NEGOTIATE OFFICIAL POLICIES?

Local programs are nested in the historical, social, and material forces that shaped Head Start, and these forces influenced how Hoover CAC administrators and Wood River staff interpreted and implemented official policies. From a historical perspective, Susan interpreted the daily-classroom-checklist policy based upon her experience at St. John's. She explained to me that the bathrooms at both St. John's and the Early Learning Center were dirty, and as was the practice at St. John's, she continued to check off that the bathrooms were cleaned daily.

Social forces, such as the change in family demographics resulting in fewer parent volunteers, influenced how Wood River staff interpreted policies. At one time staff defined local match in terms of parent volunteerism, and now, in the context of fewer parent volunteers, staff redefined the policy by counting up homework activity hours and parent donations. Staff also interpreted social changes based upon their personal histories and needs. Susan was receptive to the changes in Head Start policy toward more full-day, full-year programs because she had previous experience in child care and welcomed the opportunity to work full-time. Judy felt differently because she enjoyed having a shorter work week and having her summers free.

Material constraints, such as a federal Head Start policy prohibiting grantees from purchasing buildings with federal funds, and uncertainty about whether federal funds would be allocated for a mobile unit, limited Ann's options in finding a new location for the Wood River program and delayed a timely move to the mobile unit. This fiscal constraint can be explained in part by the long history of underfunding of Head Start programs in comparison to the funding of other high-quality and cost-effective early childhood programs.

Staff interpret and negotiate official policies and implement them in the context of local conditions, problems, and human and material resources. Policy interpretation is not fixed or finite but depends upon how staff interpret it within the context of specific and evolving events. It is at this intersection of local issues and generic policies that staff negotiate what a policy means. As the situation changes, staff may change their policy interpretations.

Two factors, perspectivity and positionality, influence how individual members of federal, state, agency, and local organizations interpret and implement policies. Perspectivity describes the view of specific individuals engaged in policy interpretation and implementation. Federal, state, agency, and local program staff, parents, and children hold different perspectives on the same policy. For instance, Ann Norstrom, the Hoover CAC Head Start director, defined the federal Head Start collaboration policy in terms of collocating local Head Start programs with other early childhood programs. From the Wood River Head Start staff's perspective, collaboration resulted in rearranging their schedule around that of the other programs at the Early Learning Center and "making do" with multiple room changes and disruptions.

How closely individuals were connected to the daily happenings at Wood River, or what was really going on, influenced how they responded to the immediate needs of the program. For instance, to the Wood River staff, operating without a divider in the gym was a major problem. Although Judy contacted the office about the divider and Martha Calle, on two visits, commented that she was "surprised the divider wasn't up yet," 4 months passed before it was installed. Judy's frustration about the difference in the Hoover CAC's perspectivity on the divider was summed up when she said, "If the office had to work like this just one day, just one day, it would go up real fast."

In a similar way, the Wood River staff's perspectivity on official federal, state, and agency policies was different from that of Hoover CAC administrators because staff were not always informed of current policies or changes in federal, state, and agency policies. Staff expected Hoover CAC to inform them of changes in policy and did not directly seek out information about policy directives. In some cases staff's unfamiliarity with official policies led to misinterpretations of local situations. For instance, Judy believed that the official policy on unexcused absences would jeopardize Allison's position in the program. However, the policy stated that when families were undergoing major changes, as was the case with Allison's parents' divorce, than the absences were deemed excused, not unexcused, and the child's place in the program was assured.

The perspectivity of other staff at Early Learning Center programs, which operated under different policies and procedures, created opportunities for both conflict and cooperative planning during the year. The special education teacher, Gale Jolly, invited Head Start to join her class for music and cooperatively planned several activities with Judy. On the other hand, Gale questioned Head Start teaching qualifications and operating procedures when she asked why Head Start teachers did not need teaching certifications and commented, after the year-long tension about the food temperature problem, "It seems that Head Start staff spend all their time on paperwork and nutrition, not that those aren't important, but are those the things that are really important? Look at how long it took to work out that thing with the lunches, that was ridiculous." From Gale's perspective, some of the activities of the Wood River staff were antithetical to providing quality programming for children and families.

Positionality is closely related to perspectivity because it describes an individual's position within a given group of people. Going back to the collaboration policy, Ann, positioned as the Head Start director, and based upon the federal team report, relocated Wood River to the Early Learning Center. Judy, positioned as the Wood River site-based manager and teacher, requested that Ann apply for a variance so that the program could remain at St. John's until funding was available for a mobile unit. However, Ann overruled Judy's request and Wood River moved to the Early Learning Center.

Staff's positionality is not unified, consistent, or easily measured. In our daily interchanges, the Wood River staff and I positioned ourselves in a myriad of ways. Our positionality could change from one interchange to the next, depending upon the context, our mood, or the subject at hand. For instance, Judy was more vocal in expressing the problems at the Early Learning Center with Wood River staff and less so with the Hoover CAC Head Start administrators. In a similar manner, when Ruth and I discussed the empty-hands-on-the-bus policy, Judy asked Ruth if she was "going to bring it up at the training." Ruth first responded that she was. Later she asked me if I thought she should bring it up. I said it was okay to bring it up, but it was up to her to decide. At the meeting, Ruth, like the other bus riders, listened unquestioningly to the description of the policy and why it was important. In the context of the local program, Ruth allowed the children to look at magazines on the bus, but in the context of the training session, and positioned as a bus rider listening to her bosses, she did not choose to challenge an established policy.

Wood River Head Start's positionality, in relation to the other programs at the Early Learning Center, created tension for the staff. From the start, the kindergarten teachers stated that Head Start could not use their playroom, and the family education program's schedule, which changed during the year, dictated the Head Start schedule and the program's access to the shared classroom. The staff were keenly aware of their second-class standing in the program and did their best to work around others. They took on housekeeping responsibilities such as bathroom and floor cleaning that staff in other Early Learning Center programs would insist be done by the janitor.

Agency administrators and local program staff highlighted some policies and downplayed others. Martha Calle, despite an agency policy prohibiting all staff from wearing blue jeans, never talked to staff about wearing jeans because she thought it was important for staff to feel comfortable sitting on the floor and occasionally getting dirty. Ann Norstrom did not tell the staff about a change in the eating policies because she did not want to stop encouraging children to try new foods. At Wood River, Ruth and Judy downplayed their understanding of the empty-hands-on-the-bus policy because they felt that it did not reflect the realities of riding the bus for four routes daily.

Both Wood River and Hoover CAC administrative staff were most familiar with the policies that applied to their everyday positions and least familiar with those more removed from their daily experiences. For example, Amanda Red, who worked with parents in completing paperwork, knew about a form granting Head Start permission to release information to public school officials. Susan and I, when approached by the kindergarten teachers for information about specific children, did not know of this form and could not consult vacationing Judy for help. When Susan called Hoover CAC for clarification, Hoover CAC administrators first told her that she could release the information and then that she could not. Confused, Susan did not know what to do until Amanda stopped by Wood River and showed her the permission form, located in each child's file.

The Wood River staff understood the need for policies to insure the health and safety of the children and staff. Gary described what it was like to drive the bus in the days before the transportation policies were enacted as a time when children sat on the floor of the van without seat belts and drivers brought children home with them when parents were not at home to receive their children. It was the prescriptive nature of some policies, such as empty hands on the bus, that set a tone of separation between the staff and administrators. Judy voiced her frustration when she talked with Ruth and me about the bus policy: "Who is making these policies, anyway? Are they the people riding the bus? I think that it should be up to the bus driver and rider. They should make the decision." She described the inherent tension in local implementation of prescriptive policies.

Head Start, like other federal programs, is subject to a "vast regulatory enterprise," and as this enterprise has grown, "rules became increasingly narrow and prescriptive" (Timar, 1994, p. 53). Narrow and prescriptive policies funnel down from the federal level to the local grantees, who in turn develop prescriptive policies for Head Start staff. Such policies require that program administrators and staff follow certain "prescriptions" to meet stated goals and objectives. Prescriptive policies result from federal mandates to document and monitor program operations and triennial reviews of grantees. For instance, in response to the findings of the 1988 federal review of Hoover CAC, Head Start administrators developed an agencywide curriculum that included required monthly and yearly topics.

Hoover CAC and Wood River Head Start staff often interpreted policy by complying with documentation and monitoring requirements. At Wood River, this compliance often took the form of procedural displays. Examples of procedural displays are staff completing the daily site inspection form and checking off that the dirty bathrooms are clean, completing lesson plans in the prescribed manner, and counting and discarding unsolicited parent donations. These displays are not reflective of the day-to-day operations of the program but rather indicate to Hoover CAC administrators that the Wood River program complied with Head Start rules.

Procedural compliance sometimes undermined the original intent of policies because the Wood River program complied with the letter but not the spirit of policies. In compliance with parent involvement policies, there were monthly parent meetings at Wood River with parent education sessions and an election of officers and representative to the policy council. However, the intent of the federal parent involvement policies, to have active parent participation in the decision making and operation of local programs and

Head Start grantees, was limited at Wood River. There, parents had little input in planning monthly meetings, choosing topics for parent education sessions, or deciding upon activities for the parent group.

During on-site visits, Hoover CAC administrators focused on completing evaluation forms developed to measure how well local programs are aligned with federal, state, and agency rules and regulations. This evaluation focus sometimes impeded administrators from assisting staff in managing the daily operations of the program, which included pressing for the installation of the gym room divider and for child-sized tables and chairs, and most important, for moving the program to more permanent classroom space.

HOW DO LOCAL STAFF NEGOTIATE POLICIES AND LOCAL NEEDS?

Head Start staff are charged with two seemingly contradictory functions: to interpret and implement official federal, state, and agency policies and, simultaneously, to serve a diverse group of parents and children with varying needs and capabilities. Martha Calle said that staff knew that children, not paperwork, are the important part of Head Start. Another Hoover CAC administrator voiced a different opinion. She said that when Hoover CAC representatives spent so much time during staff orientations and training focusing on paperwork, they gave the staff a message about what was important. Wood River Head Start staff members, under Judy's direction, recognized the importance of both attending to families and children and concurrently documenting compliance with rules and procedures.

At the start of the program year, staff observed, were observed by, and interacted with one another, the Head Start children and parents, and staff in the other programs at the Early Learning Center. Through these observations and interactions staff developed relationships with others that were vital to interpreting policies because

> the interactions of human beings lie at the heart of the education process. . . . Since relationships among human beings are by nature idiosyncratic . . . it is only a continual process of trial and error that produces effective techniques. (Gardner, 1983, pp. 368–369)

The staff then developed relationship ideas (Pauly, 1991) in the context of their interpretive understanding of official policies and their perceived need to "do something" to assist a child or family or to remedy an ongoing problem. In this trial and error process, staff, in concert with others, reformulated the policies (Pauly, 1991) to meet the needs of the children and families and solve the everyday problems they encountered.

Relationship ideas were related to the Wood River staff's personal values and beliefs. Judy, who had deep respect for parental rights, talked with parents frequently about problems and through these interchanges developed trusting relationships, such as that with Jasmine's mother, Bev, that augmented staff's efforts to support Jasmine. Judy's relationships with Sarah's and Ben's parents provided the foundation for her to negotiate speech services for the children. Judy's beliefs about children's eating and nutrition shaped how she and other staff dealt with Mark's behavior and her decision to institute a bite-of-protein policy.

In some instances, staff decided that the enactment of official policies was detrimental to the children and chose not to implement the policy. For instance, Judy did not report Allison's unexcused absences, because her interpretation of the attendance policy was that Allison could be dismissed, and she feared that Hoover CAC would withdraw Allison from the program. Judy, in deference to Bev's request to wait until Jasmine's story was made public, did not make the required child abuse and neglect report to Hoover CAC.

In other cases, staff prioritized compliance with a prescriptive policy over that of children's or parent's needs. Judy, pressed to document more and more in-kind, decided that parents' work as staff substitutes would count toward the monthly quota. In the long-standing tradition of Wood River, parents who performed staff-like functions were not offered reimbursement for their work despite a federal policy stating that parents are given priority in the hiring of staff for nonprofessional positions.

Because Head Start operated under a different administrative structure and rules from those of the other Early Learning Center programs, Judy recognized the importance of developing relationships with the staff of the other programs and simultaneously following the Head Start rules. She understood that it was important to work out the problem of the food containers in such a way that she maintained her positive relationship with Gale. Judy's conversation with the health component manager, reinforced Judy's understanding that the solution to this problem would be generated at the local level, with little support or interference from Hoover CAC. However, though Judy came up with a solution to the food problem at the beginning of the year, the food service workers did not agree to her suggestion and the problem continued until the program dietitian visited in March and ordered the food personnel to implement Judy's solution.

One explanation for Judy's lack of success in her attempt to get the food packed in separate containers and in her request that the menu be changed from the senior citizen to school lunch menu is that although site-based management increased her responsibilities, it did not delegate additional power or authority to those at the local site. Weiler (1993) contends that such policies as site-based management have a dual interest: On the one hand, they "ensure effectiveness and maintaining control" (p. 55), and on the other hand, they give the appearance that local programs have more control in daily operations. Policies such as site-based management, then, give an illusion of local control but may be enacted more for "their political utility than for their substantive viability" (Malen, 1994, p. 249). Judy voiced her understanding about the difference between the purported power and authority of site-based management and her power to make local decisions when she commented, "Sometimes with this central office, you have to get every little thing checked out. I really wonder." Judy described this juncture when she told me that often she thinks it is better to "just do what you need to do until you get caught."

The Wood River staff talked about the difference between official policies and the working policies they developed in response to the available human and material resources and working conditions. For instance, generally Ruth was successful in heating foods to the required temperature, but, despite three attempts during an inspection by the agency dietitian, she was unable to heat the foods to 160 degrees. Ruth captured the dietitian's consternation, describing the incident as "she learned there is a difference between policy and what goes on here."

Hoover CAC and Wood River staff develop practices, routines and activities that embody a local interpretation of official policy, based on their interpretive understanding of mandated policies. At the agency level, Ann Norstrom defined the official collaboration by the practice of collocating Head Start programs with other community early childhood programs. For Ann, this entailed negotiating rental agreements with school districts. At Wood River the collaboration policy resulted in the practices of collocation and cooperative planning. The practice of collocation for the Wood River staff was a year-long process that began with the move to the Early Learning Center and continued in a revamping of the Head Start schedule around that of the other programs, moving from room to room, and storing most of the program's materials and supplies.

The cooperative planning that did occur was not the result of changes in administrative structure or local policies but of relationships that developed between the Wood River staff and staff of the other programs at the Early Learning Center. Judy affirmed the value of cooperative planning, stating that until the move to the Early Learning Center she had had little contact with Gale Jolly and that one thing she would do differently in the future was to consult with her.

In viewing official policies in terms of local practices, "taken-for-granted" aspects of Head Start, such as the local-match and collaboration policies, take on different forms. The local practice of the federal-match pol-

icy is measured in empty toilet paper rolls and unwashed milk cartons. Likewise, the local practice of collocation include sharing the gym during Grace's
physical education class, storing most of the program's materials, and moving
from space to space and room to room during the day. In viewing the collaboration policy from a bottom-up perspective, Judy noted that the lesson plan
topics required by Hoover CAC hampered more cooperative planning with
other programs at the Early Learning Center. From the staff's perspective,
there were significant obstacles in increasing their cooperative activities, and
over time, cooperative activities between Head Start and the other programs
diminished significantly.

HOW DO STAFF DEVELOP LOCAL POLICIES?

Staff develop local policies by defining a problem in the context of their personal beliefs and values and their relationships and interactions with others,
trying various solutions to a problem, and developing and enforcing a policy
from practice. As local Head Start staff encountered problems, they shared
their frustrations with each other. It is through the process of ad hoc, informal networking that staff begin formulating a community-based understanding of the problem at hand. Staff's personal beliefs about children's behavior
and parenting influenced how they described and interpreted the problem.
Staff devised solutions in an interactive context by discussing the problem
and determining how to handle it based on their interactions with those involved in the problem solution. In this process, the staff "search for practical
ideas" (Pauly, 1991, p. 91) that work within the context of the program.

Through informal discussions and interactions with Mark, Jasmine, and
Bev, the Wood River staff worked toward a community understanding of
finicky eating and trauma behavior. It took staff several months to define
Mark as a finicky eater but only a few days for them to define Jasmine as the
victim of sexual abuse trauma. As they worked toward a community understanding of finicky eating and sexual abuse trauma, they tried a variety of
approaches with Mark and Jasmine. As they dealt with Mark, they used a
wider range of responses in handling his lunchtime eating behavior. However,
there was no consensus on how the staff should handle this problem, and we
tried varied solutions. As we implemented these solutions with Mark, we
learned which were successful and which were not. Mark understood that
local solutions develop in an interactive context and through trial and error
discovered that "getting sick" excused him from eating. When Judy responded by telling him that he could clear his plate, she situated in the current context her own biography of cleaning up after sick children. Mark continued to say he was sick until Judy defined a bite-of-protein policy and told

him that he would miss sledding if he got sick. Judy, Susan, and Ruth, because of their beliefs about children's eating and nutrition, thought it was important for Mark to learn to eat different foods. Over a period of time, despite my differing beliefs about children's eating, I joined the staff in enforcing this policy from practice. Mark then shifted his behavior, and despite his initial discomfort, began to try new foods.

In developing local policies to support Jasmine, the staff discussed with one another their observations about the changes in Jasmine's behavior and quickly developed consensus about her condition as a victim of sexual abuse. Judy's belief in the value of working with parents led to a meeting with Bev to elicit additional information and suggestions. From this meeting, staff developed practices that included holding Jasmine and staying with her during music classes, tolerating outbursts and misbehavior, and communicating frequently with Bev.

In several instances Wood River staff developed policies from practice that signify how they defined exemplary practice. At Wood River, Judy developed two "tiny tales of success" policies when she negotiated with the gym teacher that all Head Start children, not just those who qualified for special education services, would be included in gym class and arranged, as an outgrowth of her relationships with Gale Jolly and with parents, speech services for two Head Start children whose parents chose not enroll them in special education programs. Although those local policies may not transfer to other programs, they are hallmarks of the Wood River staff's vision of high-quality programming.

Unlike Head Start policies that are available for public inspection, policies from practice are relegated to the private realm of a particular program and are seldom recorded. Such policies are developed to meet the specific needs of a particular community of people at a designated time. Policies from practice are evaluated from the standpoint of "does it work at our local site given our situation?" Staff alter and fine-tune policies from practice as events change and new situations arise.

LESSONS FROM WOOD RIVER

Wood River has unique characteristics that distinguish it from other Hoover CAC, regional, and national programs. Studying the unique events at Wood River, however, can lead to a broader understanding of the social processes operative in other Head Start programs. What connect the unique events at Wood River to those at other Head Start programs are the historical and material forces that shape all events at local sites. Although the same events are enacted differently at other Head Start centers, the types of events are bounded by the general framework or "grammar" of Head Start.

How, then, could investigations of local policy influence the development and analysis of Head Start policy? If Head Start policy analysis included studies that investigated how local staff negotiated official policy and created policies from practice, then new understandings of policy might emerge. There are several possible outcomes. First, such research would broaden the current definitions of policy. Second, investigations could explicate how policy information is channeled from one layer of Head Start bureaucracy to another. Third, studies of local staff's interpretations of policy may result in different understandings of program quality and effectiveness. Finally, local policy studies may provide a bridge between policy makers and local staff.

Presently, the Head Start hierarchical structure, like many other federally funded programs, is predicated on national rules and regulations, not on local definitions of program quality and effectiveness. Any shift to a local approach to program quality would necessarily require that the current emphasis on procedural compliance be altered.

Prescriptive policies are based on the premises that centralized decision making and monitoring are essential when the intent is to standardize certain characteristics of local programs (Weiler, 1990), limit the risk factors in program operation, and increase program quality through prescriptive policies.

As programs attend to rule adherence they focus more on following stated rules and procedures and less on local options that might best serve children and families. This rule adherence changes the nature and scope of the program by simultaneously limiting the roles and responsibilities of program staff, radically altering the original intent of policies, and increasing the amount of paperwork and documentation required to insure that programs are in compliance. As Judy stated, program staff are spending more and more time on paperwork and, consequently, less time on providing direct services to children and families.

In this move toward zero-risk, the original mission of the program is altered as staff are undermined in their "good-faith efforts" (Timar, 1994, p. 53) to serve children and families. As staff work within a zero-risk focus, they are often frustrated by policies and procedures, such as the empty-hands-on-the-bus policy, that aim at removing rather than limiting or reducing risk to reasonable levels. Additionally, with the move toward zero-risk, agency administrators develop and enforce policy decisions that were once made by local staff knowledgeable about local conditions and needs.

I propose two changes in the current Head Start structure that would address some of the problems associated with prescriptive policies: changes in the nature of policies and changes in the evaluation and monitoring of programs. First, three different types of policies—incentive, deregulation, and pluralistic—would change the nature and scope of current practices (Pauly, 1991). Incentive policies do not mandate that programs change but reward programs that voluntarily comply with specified courses of action. Examples of Head Start incentive policies include competitive funding for programs serving families with children from birth to 3 years old. Deregulatory policies remove certain restrictions or mandates. If Head Start deregulated some of its policies, such as mandated curriculum, that make it difficult for local programs to collaborate with other community early childhood programs, then Head Start staff would be more likely to plan cooperative activities with these programs. Pluralistic policies encourage local programs to respond to program development and implementation in creative ways. These policies encourage diverse choices, create new opportunities, encourage classroom adaptation of learning methods, and provide shared support. Within this framework, local staff and parents would have more autonomy in operating their program. Programs could take advantage of new opportunities, which might include mentor teachers, assistance in developing collaborative programs, team teaching with other community early childhood professionals, and determining school calendars and operating hours in coordination with other community-based programs. Pluralistic policies recognize that each program has unique resources, diverse parents and children, and problems and that local staff and parents are best suited to fashion "solutions that are tailored to the needs of individual programs" (Pauly, 1991, p. 127). Pluralistic policies, accompanied by adequate resources allocated on the basis of local needs, unique characteristics, and teachers' requests, could change the nature and scope of local program operation.

My second proposal is a change in the nature of the Head Start monitoring evaluation system. The current system is based upon a model of complying with federal policies and mandates. Two other possibilities, proposed by Timar (1994) in response to Title I monitoring, are accreditation and inspectorate models. An accreditation system, backed up with a technical support network, would entail Head Start staff, administrators, and federal personnel inspecting and accrediting Head Start programs. Several such early childhood program accreditation systems are in place that focus on an in-depth study of local resources, strengths, and weaknesses; program improvements based upon the in-depth study, and an on-site inspection by a trained accreditation team. An inspectorate system, patterned on the British model, would year by year evaluate certain key elements of the Head Start program and produce information on the keyed areas. For instance, the inspectorate might focus on parent involvement in one year and in the following year investigate nutrition services. Such models would move the current compliance monitoring system toward a system in which programs focus more on the intent of the policies than on procedural compliance. Federal evaluation would focus on local conditions and needs and how program administrators and staff address those needs within the broad parameters of Head Start policy.

If Head Start and other federally funded programs were to move toward a mediation model that examines how local program staffs interpret and implement policies and address identified problems and needs, then it is likely that the administrative structure of Head Start grantees would also change. If Head Start administrators shifted from a monitoring toward a facilitating role, administrators might focus on how they could provide the support and resources necessary for local staff to achieve a local definition of quality and effectiveness. Administrators would "provide support for a diversity of problem-solving responses tailored to the needs and strengths of those most affected by the problems at hand" (Pauly, 1991, pp. 126–127). This shift would acknowledge that local staff are key to local program quality.

If administrators provided information on policy reform efforts and Head Start staff took a more active role in learning about and tracking policies, together they could work collaboratively within individual programs and across program staffs to envision a range of program options. This would mark a dynamic change in the current system where the "teacher's [and other staffs'] primary task is coping with change rather than enacting it" (Mintrop & Weiler, 1994, p. 272).

In creating this "unofficial" policy environment, local solutions, in addition to policy mandates, would become the mainstay of the discussion. Program staff might involve other early childhood professionals such as special education and family education staff in the discussions. As shown in the stories about Wood River, local staff often generated solutions to problems long before program monitors approved of or endorsed these same solutions.

At the heart of this policy discussion is a belief that local knowledge is a key element in quality programming. Administrators can facilitate and empower each local program in its quest for quality programming. Staffs' tiny tales of success, in addition to the items on the On-site Program Review Instrument, are the hallmarks of local program quality.

Unlike fairy tales that are told and retold in a similar fashion with each telling, stories about local Head Start programs change over time. Stories are based upon the situations at hand and are highly contextual. They change as new problems arise, as resources change, and as a new group of children enters in the fall. Staff, after all, tell and retell one another stories because "story is the very stuff of teaching, the landscape within which we live as teachers [and staff] . . . and within which the work of teachers can be seen as making sense" (Elbaz, 1991, p. 3).

Stories about programs such as Wood River, difficult to categorize because of their shifting nature, are keys nonetheless to creating a new direction for policy. They will not replace the traditional policy analysis tales, but they will augment them in critical ways. They will personalize the "nameless faces" of staff, children, and parents, and they will describe policy as it truly is practiced—in the context of the messy, idiosyncratic events at Head Start.

I believe that in these messy and idiosyncratic staff stories we may, if we listen closely enough, hear new visions of policy.

Epilogue

In the fall of 1996 the Wood River staff moved into a mobile unit adjacent but not attached to the Early Learning Center. After the unit was installed, the state fire marshal inspected the facility and ruled that it was too close to the Early Learning Center. Hoover CAC did receive a variance from the marshal so that the Head Start program could occupy the unit. The brown unit has the look of a mobile home—long and narrow, with two staircases rising from the parking lot to the structure.

Judy and Susan are glad to be in their own classroom space again, though they complain that the small unit cannot accommodate their indoor jungle gym or allow the children and staff to play circle games such as "The Farmer in the Dell." The unit contains a kitchen, two bathrooms, two tables for eating and art activities, a small circle area for story time, and shelves for blocks, toys, puzzles, games, and art supplies. Judy's husband put the shelves up high around the unit so that the staff can store supplies out of the children's reach. Judy and Susan hung brightly colored posters on the wall along with the children's artwork. There is a parent corner with resource books and handouts available to be checked out.

On my infrequent visits to the program, I noticed a change in the climate of the program—the staff and children seem more relaxed; the atmosphere lacks the stress of our frequent moves from room to room at the Early Learning Center. One day I sat with a girl and helped her make a paper chain to decorate the room for Christmas. Other children built with blocks or cooked in the play kitchen while Judy and Susan helped still others make Christmas gifts for their parents. The few children whom I recognize are younger brothers and sisters of children who attended during my volunteer years.

After years of staff's making the request, Hoover CAC agreed to the switch from the senior citizen menu to the school lunch menu. Ruth serves the lunch in the kitchen on paper plates and cups. Although the mobile unit is equipped with the three sinks necessary to comply with dish-washing procedures, Hoover CAC deemed the system inadequate and required the staff to use disposable tableware. Gary still brings the lunch for the special education program, but now he drives a new bus. Hoover CAC replaced the Wood River bus, and Gary enjoys the updated features of the vehicle.

Judy, Susan, and the children don't join Gale Jolly for music anymore or have gym class in the Early Learning Center. Those original cooperative activities are hampered because the mobile unit is not attached to the Early Learning Center and the programs still maintain their separate schedules and operating procedures. Susan created a song board like Gale's, and the Head Start staff have incorporated many features of the special education music time in their daily schedule.

Next week and in the months to come I'll stop by and visit with the staff. As Judy says, they work well together, and I always feel welcome when I make the trip to Wood River. We catch up on one another's news, laugh about the days in the Early Learning Center, and wonder about the future. I realize in these brief and infrequent visits how much I learned about policies from these seemingly ordinary Head Start staff who went about their daily business of working with children and families.

And yet a remark Judy made after reading one draft of this book lingers with me. "When I was reading this I thought, 'I really sound like a professional.' I don't think about myself that way, but that is really what I am." Judy's talk of her professional self are probably rooted in both her personal history and the current operating structure of Head Start. Unremarkable to the outside world, Judy, Susan, Ruth, and Gary are the local people who ultimately shape and define Head Start. They are the professionals who are entrusted to serve families and young children living in poverty. It is now time to acknowledge their roles as professionals and listen carefully to their untold and unheralded stories.

References

Ayers, W. (1989). *The good preschool teacher.* New York: Teachers College Press.

Barnett, W. S., & Escobar, C. M. (1987). The economics of early educational intervention: A review. *Review of Educational Research, 57*(4), 387–414.

Bereiter, C., & Englemann, S. (1966). *Teaching disadvantaged children in the preschool.* Englewood Cliffs, NJ: Prentice Hall.

Berrueta-Clement, J. R., Schweinhart, L. J., Barnett, W. S., Epstein, A., & Weikart, D. (1984). *Changed lives: The effects of the Perry Preschool Program on youths through age 19.* (Monographs of the High/Scope Educational Research Foundation, 8). Ypsilanti, MI: High/Scope Press.

Biber, B. (1979). Introduction: The preschool-education component of Head Start. In E. Zigler & J. Valentine (Eds.). *Project Head Start: A legacy of the war on poverty* (pp. 155–163). New York: Free Press.

Bissell, J. (1971). *Implementation of planned variation in Head Start I. Review and summary of the Stanford Research Institute interim report: First year of evaluation* (Publication No. OCD-72-44). Washington, DC: U.S. Department of Health, Education, and Welfare.

Black, N. (1989). *Social feminism.* Ithaca, NY: Cornell University Press.

Bloom, B.S. (1964). *Stability and change in human characteristics.* New York: John Wiley.

Bolce, D. (1990). *Informal briefing by the director of Information Services,* National Head Start Association, to the staff of the Subcommittee on Children, Family, Drugs and Alcoholism of the Committee on Labor and Human Resources, 101st Cong., 2nd sess., U.S. Senate, Washington, DC.

Bredekamp, S., & Copple, C. (Eds.). (1997). *Developmentally appropriate practice in early childhood programs serving children from birth through age 8* (Rev. ed.). Washington, DC: National Association for the Education of Young Children.

Bronfenbrenner, U. (1974). Is early intervention effective? *Day Care and Early Education, 2*(2), 14–18.

Brown, B. (Ed.). (1978). *Found: Long-term gains from early intervention.* Boulder, CO: Westview Press.

Brown, B. (1985). Head Start: How research changed public policy. *Young Children, 40*(5), 9–13.

Bruner, J. (1990). *Acts of meaning.* Cambridge, MA: Harvard University Press.

Ceglowski, D. (1994). Conversations about Head Start salaries: A feminist analysis. *Early Childhood Research Quarterly, 9*(3–4), 367–386.

Ceglowski, D. (1998). Writing short stories. In M. E. Graue & D. J. Walsh, *Children in context: Theories, methods, and ethics* (pp. 228–238). Thousand Oaks, CA: Sage.

Ceglowski, D., & Seem, J. (1994). Multiple identities and positionality in educational field research. *International Journal of Educology, 8*(2), 152–161.

Chafel, J. (1992a). Head Start: Making "quality" a national priority. *Child & Youth Care Forum, 21*(3), 147–163.

Chafel, J. (1992b). Funding Head Start: What are the issues? *American Journal of Orthopsychiatry, 62*(1), 9–21.

Cohen, D., Solnit, A., & Wohlford, P. (1979). Mental health services in Head Start. In E. Zigler & J. Valentine (Eds.), *Project Head Start: A legacy of the war on poverty* (pp. 259–282). New York: Free Press.

Cohen, D. A., & Spillane, J. (1992). Policy and practice: The relations between governance and structure. *Review of Research in Education, 18*, 3–49.

Collins, R. C. (1980). Home Start and its implications for family policy. *Children Today, 9*(2), 12–16.

Collins, R. C. (1990). *Head Start salaries: 1989–1990 staff salary survey.* Alexandria, VA: National Head Start Association.

Collins, R. C., & Kinney, P. F. (1989). *Head Start research and evaluation: Background and overview* (Report #BBB19384). Washington, DC: U.S. Department of Health and Human Services.

Consortium for Longitudinal Studies. (1978). *Lasting effects after preschool.* Denver, CO: Education Commission of the States.

Consortium for Longitudinal Studies (1983). *As the twig is bent . . . Lasting effects of preschool programs.* Hillsdale, NJ: Lawrence Erlbaum.

Coombs, F. (1981). The bases of noncompliance with a policy. In J. G. Grumm & S. L. Wasby (Eds.), *The analysis of policy impact* (pp. 53–61). Lexington, MA: Lexington Books.

Cook, A. (1994, January 19). Whose stories get told? *Education Week,* pp. 34, 48.

Coulson, J. E. (1972). *Effects of different Head Start program approaches on children of different characteristics: Report of the analysis of data from the 1968–1969 National Evaluation* (Report No. HEW-08-70-166). Washington, DC: U.S. Government Printing Office.

Council for Early Childhood Professional Recognition, (1992). *Improving child care through the child development associate program.* Washington, DC: Author.

Danziger, S., & Stern, J. (1990, September). *The causes and consequences of child poverty in the United States.* Paper prepared for UNICEF, International Child Development Center, Project on Child Poverty and Deprivation in Industrialized Countries.

Datta, L. (1971). A report on evaluation studies of Project Head Start. *International Journal of Early Childhood, 3*(2), 58–69.

Datta, L. (1972). *Planned variation: An evaluation of an evaluative research study.* Washington, DC: National Institute of Education.

Datta, L. (1982). A tale of two studies: The Westinghouse-Ohio evaluation of Project Head Start and the Consortium for Longitudinal Studies report. *Studies in Educational Evaluation, 8*(3), 271–280.

Datta, L., McHale, C., & Mitchell, S. (1976). *The effects of the Head Start classroom experience on some aspects of child development: A summary report of national evaluations 1966–1969* (DHEW Publication No. 76–30088). Washington, DC: U.S. Government Printing Office.

Denzin, N. (1994). The art and politics of interpretation. In N. K. Denzin & Y. S. Lincoln (Eds.), *Handbook of Qualitative Research* (pp. 500–515). Thousand Oaks, CA: Sage.

DeStefano, J. S., & Pepinski, H. B. (1981). *The learning of discourse rules by culturally different children in first grade literacy instruction.* Columbus, OH: Ohio State University Research Foundation.

Elbaz, F. (1991). Research on teachers' knowledge: The evolution of a discourse. *Journal of Curriculum Studies, 23*(1), 1–19.

Freeman, S. (1988). Teaching, gender, and curriculum. In L. E. Beyer & M. Apple (Eds.), *The curriculum: Problems, politics, and possibilities* (pp. 204–217). Albany: State University of New York Press.

Gardner, H. (1983). *Frames of mind: The theories of multiple intelligences.* New York: Basic Books.

Graue, M. E. (1993). *Ready for what? Constructing meanings of readiness for kindergarten.* Albany: State University of New York Press.

Gray, S., & Klaus, R. (1965). An experimental preschool program for culturally deprived children. *Child Development, 36,* 887–898.

Greenberg, P. (1990). *The devil has slippery shoes.* Washington, DC: Youth Policy Institute.

Guralnik, D. (Ed.). (1980). *Webster's new world dictionary of the American language.* New York: Simon and Schuster.

Hargreaves, A. (1994). *Changing teachers, changing times.* New York: Teachers College Press.

Harrington, M. (1962). *The other America: Poverty in the United States.* New York: Macmillan.

Head Start Act, 42 U.S.C. §§9801 *et seq.* (1994).

Hoover Community Action Council [pseud.]. (1989). *Needs assessment.*

Hoover Community Action Council [pseud.]. (1992a). *Annual report: 1992.*

Hoover Community Action Council [pseud.]. (1992b). *Policy council manual.*

Hoover Community Action Council [pseud.]. (1993a). *Head Start policies and procedures manual.*

Hoover Community Action Council [pseud.]. (1993b). *Head Start parent handbook: 1993–1994.*

Hoover Community Action Council [pseud.]. (n.d.a). *Abuse and neglect policy.*

Hoover Community Action Council [pseud.]. (n.d.b). *Food safety policy.*

Hubbell, R. (1983). *A review of Head Start research since 1970.* Washington, DC: CSR.

Hunt, J. (1961). *Intelligence and experience.* New York: Ronald Press.

Hymes, J. (1991). *Early childhood education: Twenty years in review.* Washington, DC: National Association for the Education of Young Children.

Johnson, S. M. (1994). Teachers and policy makers. *Harvard Graduate School of Education Alumni Bulletin, 36*(3), 15–17.

Katz, L. G., & McClellan, D. E. (1991). *The teacher's role in the social development of young children.* ERIC Clearinghouse on Elementary and Early Childhood Education (Catalog No. 207) Urbana, IL: University of Illinois.

Lave, J., & Wenger, E. (1991). *Situated learning: Legitimate peripheral participation.* New York: Cambridge University Press.

Layzar, J., Goodson, B., & Moss, M. (1993). *Life in preschool.* Washington, D.C.: U.S. Department of Education, Office of Policy and Planning.

Lazar, I. (1979). Social services in Head Start. In E. Zigler & J. Valentine (Eds.), *Project Head Start: A legacy of the war on poverty* (pp. 283–290). New York: Free Press.

Lazar, I., Darlington, R., Murray, H., Royce, J., & Snipper, A. (1982). Lasting effects of early education. *Monographs of the Society for Research in Child Development, 47* (2–3, Serial No. 195).

Love, J., Nauta, M., Coelen, C., Hewlett, K., & Ruopp, R. (1976). *National Home Start evaluation final report: Findings and implications.* Cambridge, MA: Abt.

Lucas, C. (1975). Problems in implementing Head Start Planned Variation Models. In A. M. Rivlin & P. M. Timpane (Eds.), *Planned variation in education: Should we give up or try harder?* Washington, DC: Brookings Institution.

Magidson, J., Barnow, N., & Campbell, D. (1976). *Correcting the underadjustment bias in the original Head Start evaluation* (Evaluation Research Reprint No. 2JM). Evanston, IL: Northwestern University Psychology Department.

Malen, B. (1994). Enacting site-based management: A political utilities analysis. *Educational Evaluation and Policy Analysis, 16*(3), 249–267.

McKey, R., Condelli, L., Ganson, H., Barrett, B., McConkey, C., & Plantz, M. (1985). *The impact of Head Start on families and communities.* Final report of the Head Start Evaluation, Synthesis, and Utilization Project.

McLaughlin, M. (1990). The Rand change agent study revisited: Macro perspectives and micro realities. *Educational Researcher, 19*(9), 11–16.

Meadows, A. (1991). *Caring for America's children.* Washington, DC: National Academy Press.

Miller, L. (1979). Development of curriculum models in Head Start. In E. Zigler & J. Valentine (Eds.), *Project Head Start: A legacy of the war on poverty* (pp. 195–220). New York: Free Press.

Miller, S. (1972). *Evaluation of the FWL Responsive Head Start Program: 1970–1972.* San Francisco: Far West Lab for Educational Research and Development.

Mintrop, H., & Wieler, H. (1994). The relationship between educational policy and practice: The reconstitution of the college-preparatory gymnasium in East Germany. *Harvard Educational Review, 64*(3), 247–277.

National Head Start Association. (1990). *Head Start: The nation's pride, a nation's challenge—Recommendations for Head Start in the 1990's. Report of the silver ribbon panel.* Alexandria, VA: Author.

National Research Council. (1976). *Toward a national policy for children and families.* Washington, DC: National Academy of Sciences.

Nauta, M. & Travers, J. (1982). *The effects of a social program: Executive summary of CFRP's infant-toddler component.* Cambridge, MA: Abt.

North, A. (1979). Health services in Head Start. In E. Zigler & J. Valentine (Eds.),

Project Head Start: A legacy of the war on poverty (pp. 231–258). New York: Free Press.

Nystrand, M., & Gamoran, A. (1991). Student engagement: When recitation becomes conversation. In H. Waxman & H. Walberg (Eds.), *Contemporary research on teaching* (pp. 40–59). Berkeley, CA: McCutchen.

Omwake, E. (1979). Assessment of the Head Start preschool education effort. In E. Zigler & J. Valentine (Eds.), *Project Head Start: A legacy of the war on poverty* (pp. 221–230). New York: Free Press.

Pauly, E. (1991). *The classroom crucible: What really works, what doesn't, and why.* New York: Basic Books.

Peters, D. (1980). Social science and social policy and the care of young children: Head Start and after. *Journal of Applied Developmental Psychology, 1,* 7–27.

Phillips, D. A., & Cabrera, N. J. (Eds.) (1996). *Beyond the blueprint: Directions for research on Head Start's families.* Washington, DC: National Academy Press.

Richardson, L. (1995). Writing-stories: Co-authoring "The Sea Monster," a writing-story. *Qualitative Inquiry, 1*(2), 189–203.

Rovner, J. (1990, April 21). Head Start is one program everyone wants to help. *Congressional Quarterly, 48*(16), 1191–1195.

Sale, J. (1979). Implementation of a Head Start preschool education program: Los Angeles, 1965–1967. In E. Zigler & J. Valentine (Eds.), *Project Head Start: A legacy of the war against poverty* (pp. 175–194). New York: Free Press.

Schön, D. (1983). *The reflective practitioner: How professionals think in action.* New York: Basic Books.

Schön, D. (1987). *Educating the reflective practitioner: Towards a new design for teaching and learning in the professions.* San Francisco: Jossey-Bass.

Schön, D. (Ed.). (1991). *The reflective turn.* New York: Teachers College Press.

Schweinhart, L., Barnes, H., & Weikart, D. (1993). *Significant benefits: The High/Scope Perry Preschool study through age 27.* Ypsilanti, MI: High/Scope Press.

Schweinhart, L., & Koshel, J. (1986). *Policy options for preschool programs.* Ypsilanti, MI: High/Scope Press.

Schweinhart, L., Koshel, J., & Bridgman, A. (1987). Policy options for preschool programs. *Phi Delta Kappan, 68*(7), 524–529.

Schweinhart, L., & Weikart, D. (1993). *A summary of significant benefits: The High/Scope Perry Preschool study through age 27.* Ypsilanti, MI: High/Scope Press.

Smith, D. E. (1990). *The conceptual practices of power.* Boston: Northwestern University Press.

Smith, M. (1973, January). *Some short-term effects of Project Head Start: A preliminary report on the second year of planned variation—1970–71.* Cambridge, MA: Huron Institute.

Stanford Research Institute. (1971). *Implementation of planned variation in Head Start: Preliminary evaluations of planned variations in Head Start according to follow-through approaches (1969–1970).* (Publication No. OCD 72-7). Washington, DC: U.S. Department of Health, Education, and Welfare, Office of Child Development.

Stone, J. (1979). General philosophy: Preschool education within Head Start. In E.

Zigler & J. Valentine (Eds.), *Project Head Start: A legacy of the war on poverty* (pp. 163–174). New York: Free Press.

Timar, T. (1994). Federal education policy and practice: Building organizational capacity through Chapter I. *Educational Evaluation and Policy Analysis, 16*(1), 51–66.

Travers, J., Nauta, M., & Irwin, N. (1982). *The effects of a social program: Final report of the Child and Family Resource Program's infant-toddler component.* Cambridge, MA: Abt.

Tyack, D. & Tobin, W. (1994). The "grammar" of schooling: Why has it been so hard to change? *American Educational Research Journal, 31*(3), 453–479.

U.S. Department of Education. (1991). *America 2000: An education strategy.* Washington, DC: Author.

U.S. Department of Health and Human Services. (1970). *Transmittal notice 70.2: Head Start policy manual. The parents* (ACYF Publication No. ACYF-IM-87-33). Washington, DC: U.S. Government Printing Office.

U.S. Department of Health and Human Services. (1992). *Head Start performance standards* (DHHS Publication No. ACF 92 31131). Washington, DC: U.S. Government Printing Office.

U.S. Department of Health and Human Services. (1993a). *Creating a 21st century Head Start: Final Report of the advisory committee on Head Start quality and expansion* (DHHS Publication No. 1994-517-593/80715). Washington, DC: U.S. Government Printing Office.

U.S. Department of Health and Human Services. (1993b). *Head Start on-site review instrument.* Washington, DC: U.S. Government Printing Office.

U.S. Department of Health and Human Services. (1997). *Project Head Start statistical fact sheet.* Washington, DC: U.S. Government Printing Office.

Van Maanen, J. (1988). *Tales of the field: On writing ethnography.* Chicago: University of Chicago Press.

Washington, V., & Oyemade, U. (1987). *Project Head Start: Past, present, and future trends in the context of family needs.* New York: Garland.

Weiler, H. (1990). Comparative perspectives on educational decentralization: An exercise in contradiction? *Educational Evaluation and Policy Analysis, 12*(4), 433–488.

Weiler, H. (1993). Control versus legitimization: The politics of ambivalence. In J. Hannaway & M. Carnoy (Eds.), *Decentralization and school improvement: Can we fulfill the promise?* (pp. 55–83). San Francisco: Jossey-Bass.

Weinstein-Shr, G. (1992). Learning lives in the post-island world. *Anthropology & Education Quarterly, 23*(2), 166–171.

Westinghouse Learning Corporation. (1969). *The impact of Head Start: An evaluation of the effects of Head Start on children's affective and cognitive development: Vol. 1. Text and appendices A–E.* Washington, DC: Clearinghouse for Federal Scientific and Technical Information. (ERIC Document Reproduction Service No. ED 036321).

White, S. (1968). The national impact study of Head Start. In J. Hellmuth (Ed.), *Disadvantaged child, Vol. 3* (pp. 168–184). New York: Brunner/Mazel.

Wolcott, H. (1990). *Writing up qualitative research.* Newbury Park, CA: Sage.

Zigler, E. (1979). Project Head Start: Success or failure? In E. Zigler & J. Valentine (Eds.), *Project Head Start: A legacy of the war on poverty* (pp. 495–507). New York: Free Press.

Zigler, E., & Anderson, K. (1979). An idea whose time has come: The intellectual and political climate for Head Start. In E. Zigler & J. Valentine (Eds.), *Project Head Start: A legacy of the war on poverty* (pp. 3–19). New York: Free Press.

Zigler, E., & Muenchow, S. (1992). *Head Start: The inside story of America's most successful educational experiment.* New York: Basic Books.

Zigler, E., Styfco, S., & Gilman, E. (1993). The national Head Start program for disadvantaged preschoolers. In E. Zigler & S. Styfco (Eds.), *Head Start and beyond.* New Haven, CT: Yale University Press.

Zigler, E., & Valentine, J. (Eds.). (1979). *Project Head Start: A legacy of the war on poverty.* New York: Free Press.

Index

Absenteeism, 89–90, 134, 138
Abuse, sexual. *See* Sexual abuse
Achievement test scores, 7
Adult-directed services, 117
Advisory Committee on Head Start Quality
    and Expansion, 9, 23, 70, 71
Agriculture Department, U.S., 76
Allison (student), 89–90, 100–101, 102, 103,
    130, 134, 138
Anderson, K., 6
Attitudes and values, 7
Ayers, W., 10, 12, 14

Barnes, H., 5
Barnett, W. S., 5
Barrett, B., 6–8
Ben (student), 63, 65, 74–75, 94, 100, 101–
    103, 130, 138
Bereiter, C., 19
Berruta-Clement, J. R., 5
Biber, B., 19
Bissell, J., 7
Black, N., 10
Blair, Donna (janitor), 50–53, 92–94
Blake, Carol (parent educator), 100
Bloom, Benjamin S., 19
Bolce, D., 24
Bonnie (student), 77
Bottom-up policy analysis, 12–13
Bredekamp, S., 56
Brian (student), 5, 15–17, 69
Bridgman, A., 5
Bronfenbrenner, Urie, 19
Brown, B., 6, 19
Bruner, J., 36
Bush, George, 23, 24–25

Cabrera, N. J., xviii
Caleb (student), 5, 85, 94

Calle, Martha (county coordinator), xvii–
    xviii, 105, 130, 133–135, 137
    dress code and, 89, 90
    gym divider and, 93, 96–97, 133–134
    parent relations and, 59–61, 69
    relocation and, 43, 45
    responsibilities, 29
    sexual abuse and, 123, 128
Camp, Grace (gym teacher), 92–95, 96, 101
Caring approach, 10
Carter, Jimmy, 23
Ceglowski, D., xix, 53, 55
Chafel, J., 24
Child abuse. *See* Sexual abuse
Child Development Associate (CDA) creden-
    tial, 22, 23
Child-Parent Centers
    as offshoots of Head Start, xiii
    tests and, xiii–xiv
Classroom capacity, 42
Clinton, Bill, 23–25
Coelen, C., 7
Cohen, D. A., 19, 35
Collaboration policy, 91, 99–104, 105–108,
    139–140, 143
Collins, R. C., 6, 7, 20, 22
Collocation, 41–58, 107, 139
    cooperative programming and, 99–104
    defined, 43
    differing experiences with, 104–105
    establishing and maintaining relationships,
    96
    facilities maintenance and, 50–53, 55–56
    negotiation of space and, 45–46, 92–95
    power distribution and, 53
    practice of, 95–99
Community of practice, 61–62. *See also* Fam-
    ilies
Condelli, L., 6–8

Confidentiality, 122–123, 127–128
Consortium for Longitudinal Studies, 7
Contributions, in local-match policy, 109–
    110, 111, 112, 114–115, 117
Cook, A., 13
Coombs, F., 11
Cooperative programming, 99–104, 139
    difficulties of expanding, 103–104
    dually serving children in, 100–102
    exploring, 106–108
    obstacles to, 105–106
    success stories in, 103
Copple, C., 56
Coulson, J. E., 7
Council for Early Childhood Professional
    Recognition, 22
Curriculum
    cooperative programming and, 99–104, 139
    developmentally appropriate practice in,
        56–58
    lesson planning and, 46–50, 51, 55
    mandated topics, 107
    parental involvement in, 70–71
    prescriptive policies, 55–56
    requirements of Hoover Community Ac-
        tion Corporation (CAC) Head Start,
        55–56

Danziger, S., 24
Darlington, R., 6
Datta, L., 6, 7, 20
Denzin, Norman, xvi, xvii, xix, 37, 133
Deregulatory policies, 143
DeStefano, J. S., 55
Deutsch, Martin, 20
Developmentally appropriate practice, 56–58
Donalds, Ruth (site aide), 4, 41, 52, 77, 88,
    118, 126, 136
    cooperative programming and, 100, 103
    empty-hands-on-bus policy and, 85–86,
        90–91, 135
    food safety policy, 98–99, 139, 147–148
    interactions with parents, 64–66
    local-match policy and, 113, 115
    profile, 33
    sexual abuse of child and, 119–129
Donations, in local-match policy, 109–110,
    111, 112, 114–115, 117
Down, Gina (parent), 65
Dress code, 27, 89, 90

Early Learning Center, 88
    collocation practice at, 41–58, 95–99, 107
    differences between programs in, 54–55
    facilities maintenance, 50–53, 55–56
    family education program, 44–45, 97, 101,
        106–108, 144
    perspectivity of staff, 133–134
    relocation of Wood River Head Start to,
        34, 36, 41–58, 91, 100
    special education program, 7, 44–45, 92–
        95, 97, 99–104, 106–108, 144
Eating policies, 73–84
    administrators and, 82–84
    basic Head Start, 81
    bite-of-protein requirement, 78, 79–84
    changes in, 89
    developing, 78–81
    finicky eaters and, 73–82
    food safety and, 97–99, 134, 138–139,
        147–148
    Hoover CAC Meal Evaluation Form, 75,
        76
    implementing, 79–81
    lunch menu and, 75–76, 138–139, 147–148
    personal experiences and, 77–79
    relational understanding and, 81–82
Education Department, U.S., 5
Education Planning Guide, 48, 49
Elbaz, F., 144
Elder, Jana (program aide), 21, 23, 25
Empty-hands-on-bus policy, 85–86, 90–91,
    135
Englemann, S., 19
Epstein, A., 5
Escobar, C. M., 5

Facilities maintenance, 50–53, 55–56
Families, 59–72
    communication with parents, 64–66, 68–69
    community of practice and, 61–62
    composition and demographics, 63, 71–72,
        133
    confidentiality and, 122–123, 127–128
    fund-raisers and, 68, 70–71
    Head Start Parent Committee, 66, 67, 70
    home visits, 65–66
    parent education, 66–67, 136
    parent meetings, 67–68, 70, 136
    parent volunteers, 64–65, 67–68, 71, 87,
        111, 112–118

power of parents and, 69–71
registration for Head Start, 63–64
right to refuse special education, 102, 103
sexual abuse and, 119–129
Family education program, 44–45, 97, 101,
    106–108, 144
Finicky eaters, 73–82, 140–141
Food. *See* Eating policies
Food safety policy, 97–99, 134, 138–139,
    147–148
Freeman, S., 9, 10
Fund-raisers, 68, 70–71

Gamoran, A., 55
Ganson, H., 6–8
Gardner, H., 137
Gender
    caring and, 10
    teaching and, 10
Gilman, E., 18, 24
Goodson, B., 8
Grade retention, 7
Graue, M. E., xvi
Gray, S., 19
Greenberg, P., 20
Guralnik, D., 43
Gym divider, 92–95, 133–134

Hall, Edward, 104
Hargreaves, A., 104–105
Harrington, M., 18
Head Start. *See also* Hoover Community Action Corporation (CAC) Head Start;
    Wood River Head Start Program
    budget of, 8–9, 24–25, 35, 114–115
    Child-Parent Centers as offshoot of, xiii
    first stage (1965–1968), 6–7, 20–21
    fourth stage (1978–present), 7–9, 23–25
    growth of, 5–6
    history of, 6–9, 15–26
    monitoring evaluation system, 143–144
    organizational chart, 18
    Performance Standards, 17, 22, 28, 29, 35–
        36, 57, 75, 76, 83, 88
    pilot project, 20
    planning for, 18–20
    policy. *See* Head Start policy
    quality of early childhood programs and,
        5–9
    reauthorization of, 54

regulation of, 136
second stage (1969–1972), 6–7, 21
statistics concerning, 5, 20, 24
summer sessions, 20, 21
teacher salaries, 21, 23, 24, 35
third stage (1972–1977), 6–7, 21–23
Head Start Act (1994), 24, 95
Head Start Bureau, 17, 22, 26, 35–36
Head Start Planned Variation Studies, 7
Head Start policy, 6, 73–84
    absenteeism, 89–90, 134, 138
    bottom-up analysis of, 12–13
    collaboration, 91, 99–104, 105–108, 139–
        140, 143
    collocation, 41–58, 95–104, 107
    downplaying, 89–90
    dress code, 27, 89, 90
    eating policies, 73–84, 89
    emphasizing, 89–90
    empty-hands-on-bus, 85–86, 90–91, 135
    examining policy implications, 90–91
    food safety, 97–99, 134, 138–139, 147–148
    growth of, 36
    history of evolution of, 6–9
    local issues in, 9–13, 131–132, 137–141
    local-match, 109–118, 139–140
    need for official, 87–88
    parents and, 66, 68–72
    policies and procedures manual, 69, 89
    staff interpretation of, 10, 132–137
    staff negotiation of, 132–140
    top-down analysis of, 11–12, 131–132
Head Start Policy Manual: The Parents, 69,
    89
Head Start Synthesis Project, 7–8
Health and Human Services Department,
    U.S., 5, 8–9, 11, 17, 21–24, 69, 70, 76,
    111, 113, 117, 131
Hewlett, K., 7
High Scope Foundation, 5
Holland, Andrea (dietitian), 80–81, 82–84,
    89, 98–99
Home visits, 65–66
Homework sheets, in local-match policy, 112,
    116–117
Hoover Community Action Corporation
    (CAC) Head Start, xv, 5, 11. *See also*
    Wood River Head Start Program
    administration of, 17–18
    Board of Directors, 28–29

Hoover Community Action Corporation
  (*continued*)
  budget, 28
  child abuse reporting policies, 122–123,
    127–128
  curriculum requirements, 55–56
  dress code, 27, 89, 90
  eating policies, 73–84
  families and. *See* Families
  food safety policy, 97–99, 134, 138–139
  history of, 20–21, 22–23, 25, 26
  local-match policy, 109–118
  monitoring of local programs, 29–30
  overview of, 28–30
  Parent Handbook, 111–112, 115
  policy determination by, 28–29, 66
  reactions to policy directives, 86–91
  registration process and, 63–64
Hubbell, R., 6
Hunt, J. McVicker, 19
Hymes, J., 24

Incentive policies, 143
In-kind, 138. *See also* Local-match policy
  described, 112
  types of, 111
Intelligence test scores, 7
Irwin, N., 7

Jacob (student), 63
Jacobs, Nora (transportation manager), 87
Jasmine (student), 77, 85, 93, 94, 100–101,
    102, 103, 130, 138
  sexual abuse of, 119–129, 140, 141
Jensen, Susan (assistant teacher), 4–5, 30
  collocation issues and, 92–94
  eating policies and, 77, 80, 81, 140–141
  Head Start policies and, 88–89, 132
  interactions with parents, 65, 66, 71
  profile, 32–33
  relocation to Early Education Centers,
    41–58
  sexual abuse of child and, 119–129
Johnson, Lyndon B., 18–20
Johnson, S. M., 83–84
Jolly, Gale (special education teacher), 42–
    43, 44, 50, 130, 138, 139
  food safety and, 97–100, 106
  music time, 16, 126, 134, 148

speech services, 102, 103, 141
  teacher credentials and, 54–55, 107
June (student), 77

Katie Lee (student)
  absenteeism of, 16–17
Katz, L. G., 125
Kevin (student), 4–5, 64
King, Lisa (parent), 65, 67–68
Kinney, P. F., 6, 20, 22
Klaus, R., 19
Koshel, J., 5

Lave. J., 61–62
Layzar, J., 8
Lazar, I., 6, 19
Lee, Katie (parent), 50–52, 67–68, 69–70
Lesson planning, 46–50, 51, 55
Lining-up procedures, 57–58
Local-match policy, 109–118, 139–140
  contributions, 109–110, 111, 112, 114–115,
    117
  described, 110–112
  documentation requirements, 111–112,
    117–118
  emphasis on written policies, 115
  homework sheets, 112, 116–117
  increases in quotas, 114–115
  local attitudes and efforts concerning,
    116–117
  policy implications, 114–118
  quotas, 112–113
  volunteer hours, 111, 112–118
Local perspective
  policy development from, 140–141
  refocusing on, 9–13, 131–132, 137–141
Love, J., 7
Lucas, C., 7
Lueck, Carla (parent), 64
Luke (student), 4, 57

Malen, B., 53, 139
Mark (student), 4–5
  as finicky eater, 73–82, 140–141
Mark, Fran (family education coordinator),
    42–46, 96
Materials, 56–57
McClellan, D. E., 125
McConkey, C., 6–8
McHale, C., 6

McKey, R., 6–8
McLaughlin, M., 7, 9
Meadows, A., 25
Mediation model, 144
Mentor teachers, 143
Meta-analysis, 7–8
Miller, L., 19
Miller, S., 7
Mintrop, H., 144
Mitchell, S., 6
Mobile unit, 43, 97, 105, 130, 133, 147–148
Monochronic time, 104
Moss, M., 8
Muenchow, S., 18–20, 22–24
Murray, H., 6
Music time, 16, 99–100, 107, 126, 134, 148

National Association for the Education of Young Children, 56
National Governors Association, 5
National Head Start Association, 8–9, 22, 23, 103
National Research Council, 18
Nauta, M., 7
Nielson, Gary (bus driver), 4, 41, 60, 88, 136, 147–148
    empty-hands-on-bus policy and, 85–86, 87
    interactions with parents, 64–66
    local-match policy and, 109–110, 115–116
    profile, 33
    sexual abuse of child and, 119–121, 125, 126–127, 128
Norstrom, Ann (Head Start director), xvi–xvii, 29, 34, 43, 76, 87–89, 88, 89, 92, 95, 97, 105, 117, 133–135, 139
North, A., 19
Nystrand, M., 55

Office of Economic Opportunity, 18, 20
Omwake, E., 19
On-Site Program Review, 33–34
Oyemade, U., 22

Parent education, 66–67, 136
Parent Handbook, 111–112, 115
Parent meetings, 67–68, 70, 136
Parents. See Families
Pauly, E., 11, 81, 137, 140, 143, 144
Pepinski, H. B., 55

Performance Standards, 17, 22, 28, 29, 35–36, 57, 75, 76, 83, 88
Perspectivity
    defined, 133
    in Early Learning Center programs, 134
    impact of, 133–134
Peters, D., 19, 21, 34
Philip (student), 5, 85, 93, 94
Phillips, D. A., xviii
Plantz, M., 6–8
Pluralistic policies, 143
Polychronic time, 104–105
Positionality
    defined, 134
    impact of, 134–135
Poverty
    of Head Start families, 63
    and quality of early childhood programs, 5
Power
    distribution of, in Head Start administration, 53
    of parents, 69–71
Practices
    collocation, 95–99
    cooperative programming, 99–104
    defined, 95
Prescriptive policies, 136, 138, 142–143
    curriculum, 55–56
    deregulatory, 143
    incentive, 143
    pluralistic, 143
Project Rush-Rush, 20

Quality of early childhood programs, 5–9
    Head Start policy analysis and, 6–9
    poverty and, 5
Quist, Luci (teacher), 25, 48

Rachel (student), 5
Reagan, Ronald, 23
Red, Amanda (family advocate), 64, 66–71, 80, 89, 122–125, 135–136
Relational understanding, 61–62, 81–82. See also Families
Report of the Silver Ribbon Panel (National Head Start Association), 23
Report on Head Start Quality and Expansion (Advisory Committee), 23
Richardson, L., 36

Roberts, Judy (site manager), xvii–xviii, 4–5,
    15–17, 25, 30
  collocation issues and, 93–94, 96
  eating policies and, 76–80, 82–84, 140–141
  interactions with parents, 60–61, 63, 65,
    67, 68–69, 71
  local-match policy and, 109–118
  parental rights and, 102–103, 122–123,
    127–128, 138
  profile, 31–32
  reactions to policy directives, 85–91
  relocation to Early Education Centers,
    41–58
  sexual abuse of child and, 122, 123–129
Room size, 42
Royce, J., 6
Ruopp, R., 7

Salaries, teacher, 21, 23, 24, 35
Sale, J., 19
Sarah (student), 5, 63, 86, 100, 101–103, 138
Schedules
  collocation issues and, 96–97
  daily, 46–53
  full day, for Head Start, 71–72, 133
Schön, D., 13
Schweinhart, L. J., 5
Seem, J., 53
Sexual abuse, 67, 119–129, 141
  defining victim of, 123
  healing process after, 125–127
  meeting with parents of child, 123–125
  policy implications, 127–129
  reporting policies, 122–123
Shay, Kathryn (parent), xvii, 31, 66–67, 70
Short, Emily (teacher), 23
Short, Jane (parent), 67, 68, 70–71
Short stories, xviii–xix
  basis for use of, xix, 36–37, 144–145
  Brian (student), 15–17
  dress code for staff, 27
  eating policies, 73–75
  empty-hands-on-bus policy, 85–86
  farm boys, 59–61
  gym divider, 92–95
  local-match policy, 109–110
  move from St. John's Catholic School, 41
  new year and, 130
  sexual abuse, 119–121
  way to Wood River, 3–5

Wood River Kwik Trip walks, 59–61
Shriver, Sargent, 18–20
Site-based management, 31–32, 53, 139
Smith, D. E., 37, 77
Smith, M., 7
Snipper, A., 6
Social competence, as goal of Head Start, 19
Solnit, A., 19
Special education, 7, 44–45, 92–95, 97, 106–
    108, 144
  cooperative programming and, 99–104
  dually serving children, 100–102
  parents' right to refuse, 102–103
Spillane, J., 35
Stand, Hope (teacher), 20–21
Stanford Research Institute, 7
Stern, J., 24
Steven (student), 4, 60–61, 63, 117, 130
Stone, J., 19
Stories. See Short stories
Styfco, S., 18, 24
Summer sessions, 20, 21
Susan (student), 5

Teachers
  licensing of, 22, 23, 54–55, 107
  salaries of, 21, 23, 24, 35
Team teaching, 143
Technical-rational perspective, 13–14
Test scores, xiii–xiv, 7
Thomas (student), 5
Timar, T., 36, 136, 142, 143
Time, conceptions of, 104–105
Tobin, W., 56
Top-down policy analysis, 11–12, 131–132
Training
  empty-hands-on-bus policy and, 90–91
  for parents, 117–118
  sexual abuse and, 128
  teacher licensing and, 22, 23, 54–55, 107
Travers, J., 7
Tyack, D., 56

Valentine, J., 18
Van Maanen, J., xix
Volunteers, parent, 64–65, 67–68, 71, 87
  conflicting policies concerning, 113–114
  local attitudes toward, 116–117
  local-match policy and, 111, 112–118

problems with, 115–116
training and, 117–118

Walsh, Daniel J.(graduate advisor), xiii–xiv,
    78–79, 82
Walsh, Paula, xv–xvi
War on Poverty, 18, 34
Washington, V., 22
Weikart, D., 5
Weiler, H., 55, 138–139, 142
Weinstein-Shr, G., 61
Wenger, E., 61–62
Westinghouse Learning Corporation, 6, 21
White, Sheldon, 6–7
Wieler, H., 144
Wohlford, P., 19
Wolcott, H., 37
Wood River Head Start Program, xvii–xix
    collocation issues, 41–58, 95–99
    daily schedule, 46–53
    daily site inspection, 50–53, 55–56
    eating policies, 73–84
    families and. See Families
    federal inspection, 33–34, 48
    history of, 20–21, 22–23, 25, 26

lesson planning and, 46–50, 51, 55
lessons learned from, 141–144
local-match policy, 109–118
mission of, 5
mobile unit, 43, 97, 105, 130, 133, 147–148
move from St. John's Catholic School, 34,
    36, 41–58, 91, 100
overview of, 3–6, 30–33
policy definition in, 131–132
power distribution and, 53
reactions to policy directives, 86–91
registration process, 63–64
relocation of, 34, 36, 41–58, 91, 100
staff interpretation of policy in, 132–137
staff negotiation of policy in, 132–140
staff profiles, 31–33
state inspection, 42
top-down analysis of, 11–12, 131–132
unique characteristics of, 12

Younger, Brenda (parent), 64

Zero-risk focus, 142
Zigler, Edward, 6, 18–20, 21–24, 26, 35–36

About the Author

Deborah Ceglowski is an assistant professor of early childhood education in the Department of Curriculum and Instruction, and outreach coordinator for the Center for Early Education and Development at the University of Minnesota. She received her doctorate from the University of Illinois at Urbana-Champaign and her master's degree from Harvard University's Graduate School of Education. In 1992 she received a Bush Leadership Fellowship to support her graduate work in early childhood education, and in 1996 she was presented with the Mary Catherine Ellwein dissertation award of the American Educational Research Association for outstanding contributions to qualitative research methodology.

Her research interests include qualitative studies of the impact of policies on teachers, parents, and children and employing alternative writing strategies, such as short stories, in writing about the impact of policies. She is presently working on a project investigating the daily experiences of families and children living in poverty. She has previously published articles on Head Start salary policies and qualitative methods.

Since 1977 she has worked with Head Start programs in consultative and teaching capacities, including 3 years in her role as a program specialist for a Head Start Support Center. Deborah has also worked in the Peace Corps and in family education, home day care, center-based day care, and nursery school programs as a teacher, parent educator, and program director.

She lives with her husband and children near Wood River, and they frequently enjoy biking and hiking in the area.